D1119225

"Drawing on Hayes's principles of acceptance and action, Mick. and Georg Eifert have produced a remarkably useful book, full of easily understood but not simplistic principles for self-change. Individuals experiencing anorexia, as well as their therapists, families, and friends can find useful wisdom in this book, reassured that it draws on new but sound principles in clinical psychology."

—Ian M. Evans, Ph.D., fellow of the American Psychological Association and Royal Society of New Zealand, and author of *Non-Aversive Intervention for Behavior Problems*

"This is an engaging and highly readable book for those hoping for a different perspective on a problem that is difficult to treat. *The Anorexia Workbook* is a life-affirming and soothing guide that teaches the art of accepting and letting go as a way to a healthy lifestyle. Rather than focusing on what is wrong, it helps the reader find the path to what is right through wonderful metaphorical images, written exercises, and active participation. I enjoyed reading this book from start to finish and learned as much about treating anorexia using ACT as about ACT itself. I actually used some of what I learned in a session with a student immediately after reading the book. This is great stuff and a gem for patients and clinicians alike!"

—Jeanne M. Walker, Ph.D., director of Psychological Counseling Services at Chapman University in Orange, CA

"This beautifully written book challenges the change agenda so often emphasized in the treatment of eating disorders. Instead, it focuses on acceptance, choice, and making commitments to living consistent with one's values and goals. The person-focused perspective, coupled with numerous examples and exercises, provide a wonderful guide for those wishing to consider an alternative to the trap of struggle and control over body image, food, and weight. The reader will find a fresh and empowering perspective on what it means to live a full, rich, and valued life and how to go about doing just that."

—John P. Forsyth, Ph.D., director of the Anxiety Disorders Research Program at SUNY, Albany

This workbook will be a great resource for people whose lives are affected by anorexia. It is easy to read, well structured, and compassionate. It takes people on a journey, helping them to travel beyond anorexia towards a more valued life path. Importantly, the workbook techniques have been supported by substantial scientific research. This book is an excellent investment and will be of benefit for years to come.

—Dr. Joseph Ciarrochi, Ph.D., senior lecturer of psychology at the University of Wollongong, New South Wales, Australia, and associate editor of Cognition and Emotion

"Michelle Heffner and Georg Eifert have done a wonderful job in applying ACT to anorexia. I believe that the practical exercises and advice in this book can certainly help people who want their lives no longer be ruled by anorexia. In particular, this book offers an avenue of hope and encouragement that is not only ultimately humane but completely different from other scientifically-driven approaches to the problem of anorexia. I have no doubt that it will transform the lives of many people."

—Frank W. Bond, Ph.D., senior lecturer of psychology at Goldsmiths College, University of London

"ACT is one of the greatest gifts I have ever received during my education and training as a doctor and general psychiatrist in private practice. ACT has the credentials of a sound scientific foundation and, as a functional approach, it allows practitioners to design highly flexible interventions with different patient populations even under the severe time constraints of a busy practice. Instead of focusing on symptoms and pathology, this treatment brings real life, values, and humanity into the doctor's office. With this marvelous book, Ms. Heffner and Dr. Eifert present ACT to the lay public for the first time. They do so in an excellent and very convincing way with a disorder that is notoriously difficult to deal with for patients and professionals alike. Highly recommended."

—Rainer F. Sonntag, MD, psychiatrist & psychotherapist in private practice in Olpe, Germany

The ANOREXIA WORKBOOK

How to Accept Yourself, Heal Your Suffering, and Reclaim Your Life

MICHELLE HEFFNER, MA • GEORG H. EIFERT, PH.D.

Foreword by Steven C. Hayes, Ph.D.

New Harbinger Publications, Inc.

Contents

Foreword
    Starting from Here   vii

Acknowledgments   ix

Introduction   1

PART 1
UNDERSTANDING ANOREXIA

CHAPTER 1
    What Is Anorexia?   9

CHAPTER 2
    An Anorexia Self-Test   25

PART II
TREATING ANOREXIA WITH ACT:
Change What You Do, Not What You Think and Feel

CHAPTER 3
    Accept—Choose—Take Action: *The Basics of Acceptance and Commitment Therapy*   35

CHAPTER 4
When Control Gets Out of Control   47

CHAPTER 5
Learning to Be a Mindful Observer   61

CHAPTER 6
Approach Difficult Situations with Acceptance   79

CHAPTER 7
Choosing Valued Directions   93

CHAPTER 8
Staying Committed to Valued Living   117

CHAPTER 9
Emily's Journey to Recovery   129

PART III
PROFESSIONAL TREATMENT ISSUES

CHAPTER 10
Professional Treatment Options   141

CHAPTER 11
Established Psychological Treatments For Anorexia   151

CHAPTER 12
Preparing for Treatment with a Therapist   159

PART IV
ADDITIONAL RESOURCES

CHAPTER 13
A Chapter for Loved Ones   171

CHAPTER 14
Assess Your Progress   185

References   195

Foreword

Starting from Here

Why do humans suffer so? This has been a puzzle for as long as humans have wondered about it. There have been many answers. One superficially appealing answer is that life is simply too hard, and that what we need is more ease, time, stimulation, conveniences, appliances, parties, and so on. But as human beings have learned better and better ways to make life easier, many problems have become worse. As science and technology provide conveniences, they also feed an implicit underlying message, namely that feeling good is the measure of a human life.

In most areas, "feel good-ism" has multiple manifestations. They may look quite different, but at their root they are the same. For example, a person who is anxious may indulge the anxiety and "do what it says" to get it to go away. For instance, anxiety might tell the person, "run and stay away from situations that make you feel anxious" and the person might do so. At other times, the same person may try to suppress the anxiety directly (for example, through alcohol, drugs, or obsessive rituals) to get it to go away. Underneath both forms of adjustment is the same basic pattern: turning one's life over to thoughts and feelings, even when the behavior that results is not workable, caring, or healthy. It is like a child who resists or complies with requests from a parent: the two patterns look quite different but in both cases the commands from the parents are in control of the child's behavior.

Food presents much the same picture. On the one hand, we have rising rates of indulgence and obesity, and on the other hand there is an ever increasing number of people with eating disorders. Sometimes, both patterns occur within a single individual (for example, the bingeing and purging of bulimia). But in all these examples, the individual has allowed thoughts and feelings about food to take control of her behavior.

ACT takes another approach altogether. Instead of trying to change one's thoughts and feelings first, ACT tries to change the way people respond to their thoughts and feelings—especially how one behaves in the presence of them. Instead of trying to get all of our thoughts lined up in a row, ACT teaches us how to watch our thoughts—gently, with dispassionate interest, without entanglement—*and* to do what needs to be done in a given situation.

In this book, Michelle Heffner and Georg Eifert invite you to walk with them down this new path. Where there once was avoidance, they help create acceptance. Where there once was entanglement with your thoughts and feelings, they help create mindfulness. Where there once was desperation and meaninglessness, they help create valued action.

ACT does not promise that difficult thoughts and feelings will go away. Sometimes they do. Sometimes they don't. What it does promise, however, is that every human life can be dignified, valued, and whole—with pain when there is pain—and yet alive, real, healthy, and honest. Most of all, it suggests that this process can start from here, right now. Instead of starting from where you are *not* (feeling and thinking differently, so that different behaviors can eventually occur), ACT suggests starting from where you *are*, with your thoughts, feelings, memories, behavioral predispositions, and bodily sensations that are already there.

The research programs on the benefits of this approach are still young, but they are growing. Research teams around the world are documenting the benefits of acceptance, mindfulness, and valued action. These approaches are barely visible in the mainstream culture, and they can be confusing, subtle, and hard to express in words. I think the authors have done a masterful job of putting ACT into a form that people may be able to use directly. For those who have struggled and failed with existing approaches, ACT presents an alternative path. If you are willing, this book will help you walk that path and to discover whether this new approach will empower you to show up, let go, and reconnect with your commitment to live a healthier and more humane lifestyle.

—Steven C. Hayes
University of Nevada

Acknowledgments

I would like to acknowledge my clinical supervisors Jeannie Sperry, Scott Mizes, Lisa Hamilton, Jan Melcher, Peter Kahn, Lynda Danley, and Barry Edelstein. This book is a culmination of the excellent training you have provided to me, and I hope you recognize that your influence is reflected in this work. Thank you for sharing your expertise with me.

—Michelle Heffner, MA

I thank my good friend and colleague, Laurie Ann Greco, for exploring with me what acceptance and mindfulness mean in our daily lives, and for studying and writing about ACT with me. I also thank my friend, colleague, and mentor, Ian Evans, without whose influence and support I would not have pursued the path I have chosen. I am very grateful to Pema Chödrön (a Buddhist nun), and to the dear client who introduced me to her writings, for helping me understand the importance of seeking out the "places that scare you." Finally, I thank and acknowledge Diana Monroy, who has lived ACT since long before I ever knew anything about it and whose humility and exuberance inspire me every day. Her life serves as a reminder to me of how much people can achieve if they don't give up and strive to live their dream in the face of prolonged, uncontrollable adversity.

—Georg H. Eifert, PhD

Acceptance and commitment therapy (ACT) is new. It is evolving literally every day through open exchanges on the Internet and through journal articles and book chapters. These writings and ideas are shared with colleagues and sometimes posted on the Internet years before they will get published and copyrighted. We both are extremely grateful to Steven Hayes and Kelly Wilson, who have generously made their work and ideas available to us in the spirit of "free sharing and spreading of what is good." Unfortunately, this is not always done in science, which makes Steven's and Kelly's generosity and great support stand out even more.

We also thank the following professionals and organizations who gave us permission to reproduce their work: John Blackledge, Frank Bond, John Bush, Scott Mizes, the Association for Advancement of Behavior Therapy (AABT), and The Guilford Press. Finally, we are very grateful to Catharine Sutker from New Harbinger for her continuous and strong encouragement to move ahead with this project and to Heather Mitchener for her masterful and diligent editing.

Introduction

A few years ago, a teenaged girl named Emily reluctantly entered our clinic, feeling pushed into treatment by her concerned mother. Emily had anorexia. She was very thin, and she did not want to eat. At that first meeting, we could never have imagined that Emily would go through a groundbreaking recovery that would eventually lead to the publication of this workbook. Her journey toward a valued life beyond anorexia is presented in chapter 9.

What makes Emily's case stand out is that her recovery became the first published account of the effectiveness of *acceptance and commitment therapy* (ACT) in treating anorexia (Heffner et al. 2002). We first published Emily's story in a professional journal to educate other psychologists about ACT as a promising approach to treating anorexia. The reaction to this article was very positive.

Since publishing Emily's treatment story, we have used ACT to treat more clients with anorexia and other eating disorders. When we were offered the opportunity to write this workbook, we enthusiastically accepted, because there is growing evidence that ACT works, and we want to spread this message to those who need to hear it most: The hundreds of thousands of people who struggle with anorexia every day.

What Is ACT?

Psychologist Steven Hayes and his colleagues Kirk Strosahl and Kelly Wilson developed acceptance and commitment therapy (ACT), which is pronounced "ACT" in one word, not A-C-T as separate letters. This pronunciation is important because it summarizes what ACT ultimately stands for: committed action.

ACT can be used for all kinds of psychological problems, and we adapted it to help people with anorexia. ACT may not be a household word, but its recognition is growing. For example, ACT was featured as an innovative therapy approach in an August 2002 article published in *O.*, Oprah Winfrey's magazine.

There are essentially two important components to ACT: (1) acceptance of the uncontrollable thoughts and feelings you experience and (2) commitment and action toward living a life that you value. So this workbook is about acceptance *and* it is about change at the same time. You will learn to accept and live with the uncontrollable thoughts and feelings that haunt you about your weight, and you will learn to take charge and move your life in directions that you value.

The philosophy of ACT is somewhat similar to the serenity creed that you may already be familiar with: *"Accept with serenity what you cannot change, have the courage to change what you can, and develop the wisdom to know the difference between the two."* Many people love this creed. You'll see these inspirational words displayed on refrigerator magnets, desk plaques, and wall frames.

Yet despite these daily reminders, most people simply do not know what they *can* change and what they *cannot* change. It seems much easier to agree with the serenity creed than to do what it says. As a result, some people become frustrated with the serenity creed because they do not know how to apply this profound statement to their daily life. With this workbook, you will learn how to live by the serenity creed on a daily basis and turn this wisdom into real action.

Part II of this workbook will help you put the serenity creed into action. In chapter 3, we provide an overview of ACT, followed by a step-by-step presentation of ACT techniques in chapters 4, 5, 6, 7, and 8.

As you progress through the ACT program, you will learn to:

- Recognize that trying to control and change what you feel and think about yourself by losing weight is risky and does not work

- Deal with out-of-control emotions, thoughts, and situations more effectively

- Identify what you value in life and what you want your life to stand for

- Take steps toward leading a valued life

- Cope with barriers that stand in the way of your dreams

Make This Workbook Work for You

To get the most of out this book, make reading a priority in your schedule. Commit to a reasonable amount of time that you can set aside to read this workbook and practice the exercises.

Commitment is a central component of ACT. Chapter 7 includes a weekly planning calendar. You may want to copy this planner now and devote specific times in your daily schedule to reading and working with this workbook. Put taking care of yourself on your to-do-list each day. Reading this workbook is a great self-care activity.

Each chapter includes worksheets and exercises. The exercises are the most important parts of this workbook because they allow you to apply the treatment techniques to your personal life. There is a good chance that this book will help you and work for you, but only if you commit to it. It is up to you to make it work for you!

However, if you do not complete the exercises, nothing much is going to change in your life—or as ACT founders Hayes, Strosahl, and Wilson (1999) say, *"If you always do what you always did, you will always get what you always got"!* (p. 235) So it will be up to you to put what you learn into action and make the changes you need to make.

Who Is This Book For?

We've written this book for one main audience and two secondary ones:

People with Anorexia

If you feel driven to be thin, are afraid of gaining weight, and restrict how much you eat, you have selected the right book. This book is written directly for you. In chapter 1, we provide an overview to help you learn more about the symptoms, causes, effects, and treatments of anorexia.

Because the vast majority of people with anorexia are female, we use feminine pronouns (she/her) throughout this book. Please note, however, that this book is directed at *anyone* who suffers from anorexia, regardless of gender. Males with anorexia can benefit from ACT just as well.

Family and Friends

Families and friends are very concerned when someone close to them develops anorexia. They wonder if they did something to cause the disorder, and they struggle with what to say and what to do. At times, they may even worry about whether their loved one will die.

Chapter 13 is devoted specifically to family members, and we hope this chapter will answer questions and guide your friends and family to best support you. If you are a person experiencing symptoms of anorexia, you might want to give a copy of chapter 13 to someone close to you. Loved ones also may be interested in reading the overview of anorexia we present in chapter 1.

Professionals

Therapists know how difficult it is to help people with anorexia. The situation is especially difficult because there are no step-by-step treatment manuals for anorexia. We hope this book can provide a helpful structure that clinicians can follow to help people with anorexia transform their lives. The step-by-step format of this workbook can be used in group and individual therapy formats.

Clinicians may want to suggest this workbook to clients as recommended reading, because there are few self-help books written by professionals directly for the person with anorexia. We also encourage professionals to use this book as a treatment protocol to gather and publish outcome data to provide further empirical support for ACT, a novel approach to the treatment of anorexia.

How Can This Book Help You?

If you are seeing a professional, we encourage you to share this workbook with your therapist. It will help your therapist to know what type of treatment approach you would like to receive. Your therapist might also be able to provide you with some added professional input as you progress through the ACT program. Even if your therapist is using a somewhat different treatment approach, this workbook can still work for you and help you behave in ways that are in line with your chosen values and that bring you closer to goals you can set for yourself.

Finally, this workbook reaches out to the many people with anorexia who are not participating in professional treatment for whatever reason. Perhaps you recognize your own situation in one of the categories below.

You Think Therapists Will Force You to Eat

We want to reach out to those who do not want to see a therapist because they suspect that therapists are only interested in getting them to eat more to gain weight. If this describes you, we want you to understand one thing: *This workbook is not about getting you to eat more.* Our workbook contains no guidelines or recommendations on how much you should eat and how much you should weigh. We believe you basically know all this because you have heard and read it a million times. So we will not bug and nag you about dietary requirements.

This workbook is not about getting rid of anorexia, as odd or unbelievable as that may sound. This workbook is about reclaiming your life. In the end, you may decide that you need to eat healthier to be physically strong enough to move your life in directions that you value. Ultimately, you are in control of what direction you want your life to take. That is your choice. Neither this book nor anyone else can force you to live your life in a certain way. In ACT, weight gain is not the main focus of treatment. Eating is merely a means to a valued end. It is not *the* end or goal.

It Is Difficult for You to Access Treatment

Some people live in locations where it is difficult to find professional treatment for anorexia. Some live in small cities where none of the practicing psychologists are eating disorder specialists. Others live in rural parts of the country where few psychological services are available at all.

We served clients in the rural state of West Virginia for a number of years, and we understand how difficult it is for clients to drive several hours to a clinic. The one-hour therapy session can easily turn into a daylong journey. For some people, travel is expensive and time-consuming. For others, travel is not possible at all. We hope this book transcends any distance barrier you experience and inspires you to take control of your life like a weekly meeting with a therapist might (or even more!).

You Feel Professional Treatment Is Too Invasive

Some people prefer to work with a self-help book because working with a book is less invasive than therapy. We know it can be embarrassing or scary to reveal your most personal and sensitive problems to a stranger who will be your therapist.

Regardless of the specific reason why you may not want to see a therapist, we hope this book will help you move your life in directions that you value. At the end of the book, you may decide that you are heading in the right direction and that you may not need any further professional treatment. On the other hand, you can also use this book as preparation for working with a professional at a later time if you think you still need to or prefer to do that. Chapters 10, 11, and 12 are devoted to treatment issues. Read these chapters to learn what to expect if you eventually decide to seek professional treatment.

Hopefully, your experience with this workbook will help you feel more confident about working with a professional.

Begin Your Journey

There is a Buddhist saying that the journey of a thousand miles begins with one step. By selecting this workbook, you have taken that first step on your journey toward recovery. Congratulations!

There are many more steps to take, and now is the time to keep moving forward. Living according to your values is a lifelong pursuit. On your journey, you will continuously learn, progress, and see life in a way that you may never have experienced before. You can look at this workbook as a travel guide that provides information to help you decide where you want your journey to take you.

Now it is time to take off . . .

PART 1

UNDERSTANDING ANOREXIA

CHAPTER 1

What Is Anorexia?

In this chapter you will learn to:

* Assess whether you have anorexia

* Understand the different types of anorexia

* Understand the different causes of anorexia

You Are Not Alone

You may have told yourself, "I feel so alone. My problem is too hard to talk about because no one understands." As you read through this chapter, we hope you discover the facts about anorexia: the symptoms, causes, and effects of this eating disorder. One of the most important facts we want to convey is that you are not alone. Other people share your fears, behaviors, and feelings. Many of the clients we treat feel a sense of relief when we present them with the facts you are about to learn. We hope you too will discover that your problem is indeed recognized and understood. It's crucial to remember: You are not alone!

At present, we know that the vast majority of people who suffer from anorexia are female. However, there is a small, but growing number of males with the disorder. Most people develop anorexia during their teens. Some recover in a relatively short period of time, but we have worked with several middle-aged clients who have struggled with anorexia for decades. There are also some people who develop anorexia as adults, usually in reaction to an upsetting life event, such as divorce or trauma.

It is impossible to determine exactly how many people have anorexia because some hide or deny their symptoms and avoid seeking treatment. Research surveys from Europe and the United States show that in a group of 100 women, approximately one has anorexia (American Psychiatric Association 2000). That amounts to 1 percent of women and may not sound like a large number. Yet when you consider the size of the population, 1 percent adds up to a huge amount of suffering for a lot of people. Surveys also show that the number of people who have problems with anorexia has been rising dramatically in the past twenty to thirty years.

The Diagnosis of Anorexia Nervosa

Only a trained professional can diagnose anorexia, but the following section can provide you with an overview of the types of symptoms a professional would look for. To be diagnosed with anorexia, a person must experience the following symptoms:

- Fear of weight gain

- Body image dissatisfaction

- Extremely low body weight

- Three consecutive missed menstrual cycles

In the next chapter, you will have a chance to complete a detailed questionnaire to help you assess in more detail some of your thoughts, worries, and attitudes about eating, the way you look, and what other people think of you. At this point, we ask you to simply place a check mark in the list below next to the symptoms you experience. This will give you a better idea of how closely your current situation resembles that of other people with anorexia.

Remember, the idea is not to establish whether you should be diagnosed with anorexia. Only a professional can do that. Instead, we would like to help you assess how many of the critical symptoms you experience. The more check marks you make, the more likely anorexia is a significant problem for you:

Anorexia Checklist

_____ Do you have an intense fear of weight gain?

_____ Do you feel an overwhelming need and drive to be thin?

_____ Do you need to be thin to feel good about yourself?

_____ Do you perceive yourself as fat, even though others do not think you are?

_____ Have you missed at least three consecutive menstrual cycles? This criterion does not apply to males, females who have not had their first period, postmenopausal women, and those taking birth control pills.

_____ Is your body mass index (BMI) less than 18? You can use the box and formula below to calculate your BMI.

Calculate your body mass index or BMI using the formula in the box below. The BMI is a common way to measure how much you weigh in relation to your height.

Doctors and researchers rely on the BMI because it is the best way to determine how overweight or underweight a person is. If you assess weight in pounds alone, you are not accounting for height. For example, two people could each weigh 100 pounds, but the person who is 5'5" would be more underweight than a person who is 5'3."

The healthy range for the BMI is 20-25. A BMI from 26 to 30 is considered overweight, and above 30 is considered obese. A BMI of 18-19 is considered borderline and a BMI of less than 18 is considered underweight.

Is your BMI less than 18?

Calculating Your BMI

What is your height *in inches*? _____

Be sure to convert feet to inches by multiplying feet by 12 and then adding inches.

Example: If you are 5 feet, 2 inches your height in inches is 62 (5 x 12 = 60; 60 + 2 = 62)

What is your weight in pounds? _____

Now plug the number above into the following formula:
[Weight in pounds ÷ Height in inches ÷ Height in inches] x 703

Example: if you are 5'2" (62 inches) and weigh 115 lbs, your BMI is:
[115 ÷ 62 ÷ 62] x 703. This equals 21, which is in the healthy range.

If you prefer to use the metric system, you can calculate your BMI using the following formula: Weight in kilograms ÷ [Height in meters^2]

Example: Let's assume you weigh 42 kg and your height is 1.62 m (162 cm)
42 ÷ [1.62 x 1.62]. This equals 16, which is below the healthy range.

The Two Types of Anorexia: Restricting versus Binge-Purge

Are you experiencing some of the symptoms described in the list above? If so, the next step is to identify which type of anorexia is consistent with your behavior. Please note that there are two types of anorexia: one is called the *restricting type* and the other one is referred to as the *binge-purge type*. Those diagnosed with restricting type limit how much they eat. Those diagnosed with binge-purge type restrict calories too, and they also force themselves to throw up, exercise excessively and/or abuse laxatives, diet pills, or diuretics.

Those with binge-purge subtype believe that purging reduces caloric intake. That belief is not accurate and probably the result of a lack of understanding of what happens with food once it is eaten. Except for exercise, which really does burn calories, the other techniques that are often used do not work well because calories are absorbed very quickly. This is the main reason why purging does not really work as a weight control method.

We like to explain this fact by using a hot stove metaphor. Calories, like heat, are a form of energy. If you've ever touched a hot stove, you know that heat energy is absorbed very quickly (and painfully) once your hand hits the stove. Likewise, once food is eaten, the calories are absorbed rather quickly. If a person who engages in purging techniques loses weight, it is usually by coincidence, with weight loss due to caloric restriction or increased exercise, not purging.

Other Types of Eating Disorders

Apart from anorexia, there are other patterns of eating behavior that are considered problematic from a psychological perspective. Let's briefly review them.

Bulimia

The binge-purge subtype of anorexia is often confused with another eating disorder, bulimia nervosa. Bulimia is an eating disorder where an individual experiences body image concerns, consumes an excessive amount of food, and then purges to "undo" the overeating (e.g, through vomiting, excessive exercise, fasting).

The two main distinctions between the binge-purge type of anorexia and bulimia are binge quantity and body weight. First, a person with bulimia binges on truly excessive amounts of food—typically junk food. They eat much more than most people would eat under similar circumstances. In contrast, what a person with anorexia considers a binge is quite subjective and would not even be considered a binge by most other people. For instance, a person with anorexia might consider having one large milkshake excessive, although most people would not regard this as a binge. On the other hand, a bulimic person might have four milkshakes in a row, which even big eaters would probably regard as excessive. Also, due to the excessive caloric intake during a binge, people with bulimia tend to be of normal weight or slightly overweight, whereas people with anorexia are severely underweight.

Eating Disorder, NOS

Eating Disorder, Not Otherwise Specified is a diagnosis used to describe people experiencing problems with eating and weight who do not have all of the symptoms of a specific eating disorder. For example, one of our clients, Carrie, restricted her caloric intake to 1000 calories per day and had an intense fear of weight gain. Her BMI was 20 and her menstrual cycle was regular. Although some of Carrie's symptoms closely matched some of the diagnostic criteria for anorexia, her BMI was still in the normal range and her menstrual cycle was regular. Therefore she was diagnosed with Eating Disorder, Not Otherwise Specified.

This was an ideal time for Carrie to start a treatment program because she started to do something about her problem before her symptoms had progressed to a more severe level. Carrie's case illustrates why this workbook is helpful not only for those who meet all diagnostic criteria for anorexia, but also for those readers who have some of the symptoms but not all of them (yet). If you fall into this category, you may be able to prevent things from getting worse by embarking on the ACT program we describe in this workbook.

Ultimately it does not really matter whether you meet some or all of the diagnostic criteria for anorexia. So you can relax about the diagnosis issue. What *is* important is to simply recognize and acknowledge that you have a problem with your eating and your drive to be thin, that you want to deal with the problem in a way that moves your life forward, and that you are willing to try out a new approach to dealing with your concerns about being too fat or not thin enough.

You Are Not "An Anorexic"

Many people fall into the language trap of referring to themselves as "an anorexic." Unfortunately many doctors use the same language and jargon. We encourage you to stop labeling yourself as an anorexic because it sends the wrong message to you and the people around you. Giving up this kind of language will help you stop the endless psychological battles you have been fighting.

You are a person first, and the way you describe yourself is very important. There is a big psychological difference between saying: *I am anorexic* and *I am a person who has a problem with anorexia.* This second version may sound odd, and it definitely is more cumbersome. Yet this change in how you describe yourself is more than just a wording change. By calling yourself an anorexic, you make yourself and the problem one and the same, almost as if all you are is anorexia.

Does anorexia define you? Is that how you want to define yourself? We realize that you may sometimes feel you are anorexia because you are consumed with your fears about weight and your desire to be thin. The good news is: *You are much more than an eating disorder.* First and foremost, you are a person, a human being, with a lot of potential to become and do whatever you choose to do.

One of the goals of ACT is to show you that you are definitely more than a "disordered person." As you progress through the ACT program, we will show you how you can have thoughts and feelings about being too fat *and* live a valued life at the same time. Your thoughts and feelings related to anorexia do not have to rule your life and stand in the way of your dreams.

Through ACT, you will learn that language can be very powerful. The words we use can be quite destructive and trap us into corners that are difficult to get out of. That is why subtle changes can lessen the destructive impact of language and make a big difference in helping you move forward in a valued direction where you truly want to go.

Another Example of the Language Trap

Just as there is a big difference between saying, "I am an anorexic," and, "I am a person with a problem called anorexia," there is also a difference between saying: "I am fat," and, "I am having the thought that I am fat."

"I am fat" is a factual statement and it makes you and fat one and the same thing. If you say, "I am fat," then you become what your thoughts tell you to be. Your thoughts and you melt into one piece and trap you.

If you said instead, "I am having the thought that I am too fat," you make an important difference between who you are, a person, and your thoughts of how you evaluate yourself.

Again, we know this sounds awkward, but if you start describing your thoughts in this cumbersome way, it will help you create an important distance between yourself and your evaluations of yourself. We'll keep stressing this point throughout this workbook.

Other Conditions that Mimic Anorexia

Some people experience symptoms that resemble anorexia, but when we take a closer look we discover that these people don't really have anorexia. Instead, they suffer from medical problems or depression.

Medical Conditions

There are some people who maintain very low body weights and report no other symptoms of anorexia. They eat regularly, and they do not understand why they are so underweight. They report no body image concerns or weight gain fears. In fact, some of them want to gain weight because they don't like being thin.

These cases do not fit the presentation of anorexia, and we always recommend that the individual see their medical doctor to determine if an underlying medical condition is causing weight loss. For example, some people suffer from hyperthyroidism, which is an excessive amount of thyroid hormones circulating in the blood because of an overactive thyroid gland. The physical effects of hyperthyroidism include weight loss, hair loss, and loss of sex drive. Although these symptoms appear very much like anorexia, they are caused by an overactive thyroid gland. Likewise, many gastrointestinal disorders can cause digestion problems and weight loss.

So if your only symptom is low body weight, and you do not experience weight-gain fears, intense desire to be thin, or body image dissatisfaction, we urge you to see your doctor immediately because you probably do not have anorexia. Instead, you may have a medical problem that should and can be treated by your family doctor.

Depression

Anorexia and depression share many similar symptoms such as social withdrawal, fatigue, concentration problems, and weight loss. Due to this overlap, it can be difficult for psychologists to determine if a client has anorexia, depression, or both. If a client has experienced a recent weight loss, the best way to distinguish between anorexia and depression is by examining why a person has stopped eating.

In depression, people lose their appetite and food no longer tastes good. The depressed person stops eating because of a loss of interest in food rather than intentional dieting to prevent weight gain. On the other hand, a person with anorexia remains interested in food and usually feels hungry, but stops eating due to the intense fear of weight gain. People with anorexia also have an intense drive and desire to be thin that is not common in people with depression. In fact, depressed people lack the drive to do anything at all.

Although anorexia and depression are separate disorders, it is possible for an individual to have both disorders at the same time. In fact, depression and anorexia can contribute to each other in several ways. In some cases, people become depressed as a result of having anorexia. Studies have shown that when people restrict their diet for a period of time, they become more irritable and they prefer time alone over social interaction. They have less energy to do anything. As a result, they have fewer opportunities for socialization and pleasant experiences, which leads to feelings of depression.

In other cases, depression leads to anorexic behavior. Depression occurs when people experience an imbalance of positives and negatives in life. They lose touch with the positive aspects of life and feel burdened and overwhelmed by the negatives. When life's negative events outweigh the positive events, we feel we have lost control. At that point, anorexia can develop as a way to regain control in an out-of-control world. We often hear clients say, "I can't control anything else in life. At least I can control my weight."

Psychological Disorders That Co-Occur with Anorexia

Depression is not the only disorder that can co-occur with anorexia. Many people with anorexia live through stressful conditions that predispose them not only to eating problems, but also to other types of psychological conditions. In this section, we will review some of the other psychological conditions that commonly co-occur with anorexia. This ACT workbook can still work for you even if you have multiple problems. Although we focus on anorexia, the ACT approach is useful for a variety of different disorders, not just anorexia. You can relate what you learn about ACT to help you deal with these other problems as well.

Obsessive-Compulsive Behavior Patterns

Are you a perfectionist? Are you a person who is driven to be perfect, maintains extreme orderliness, rigidly follows rules, and feels an intense need to be in control? This obsessive-compulsive personality style can interfere with your interactions with other people and can cause you to overreact to failures and mistakes. When this personality style and anorexia occur together, it is most likely to occur in a person with anorexia of the restricting type.

It is also possible for people with anorexia to have symptoms of *obsessive-compulsive disorder* (OCD). OCD is an anxiety disorder in which individuals feel compelled to engage in endless rituals to reduce disturbing and frightening thoughts that they feel unable to stop. Some people with anorexia do not meet the actual diagnostic criteria for OCD but still engage in pervasive patterns of obsessive-compulsive behavior. For instance, some may set rigid rules for food preparation, cut food into specific shapes, or engage in a variety of ritual behaviors to rid themselves of unwanted thoughts that are focused on gaining weight.

Post-Traumatic Stress Disorder (PTSD)

Have you experienced a situation in which you felt that your life or the life of someone you loved was threatened? This includes situations in which people feel helpless and afraid, such as natural disasters, sexual assaults, witnessing a crime, or car accidents.

Among women, sexual assault is the most commonly reported type of traumatic event (Kessler et al. 1995). Most people think of forcible rape when they hear the word sexual assault. However, sexual assault does not always mean a violent attack. Anytime someone touches you sexually against your will, it is considered sexual assault. Psychologists are interested in knowing how many women with anorexia have been sexually abused. One study found that 50 percent of women hospitalized for anorexia had been sexually abused (Hall et al. 1995). That means that the rate of sexual abuse is very high among women hospitalized for anorexia, especially when compared to rates of sexual abuse among women without eating disorders in the general population, where only 7 percent report being sexually abused (Deep et al. 1999).

Post-traumatic stress disorder (PTSD) is a response to being in a traumatic, life-or-death situation. People with PTSD re-experience the trauma through frightening flashbacks and memories and avoid talking or thinking about what happened. In many cases, they seem to be on edge constantly. They are on-guard at all times and experience anger outbursts. A group of researchers (Gleaves, Eberenz, and May 1998) found that 74 percent of patients hospitalized for an eating disorder had experienced a traumatic event in their life. Of those who experienced a trauma, 52 percent developed all of the symptoms of PTSD. McFarlane, McFarlane, and Gilchrist (1988) explained that people who experience a traumatic event can develop anorexia because weight control reduces the feelings of helplessness and victimization.

Consider the case example of Kelly, a twenty-year-old who was sexually assaulted by a male acquaintance. She developed symptoms of PTSD. When her assailant was acquitted in court for lack of evidence, Kelly's symptoms became worse. She felt ashamed and helpless. She attempted to overcome or at least reduce these feelings and regain control of her life by controlling how she looked and how much she ate. At first, anorexia seemed to empower her. Kelly continued to fast and abuse laxatives. Her weight dropped from 140 pounds to 86 pounds.

At that point, Kelly realized that anorexia was not a solution—it was a problem. She was not really controlling her weight anymore. Her weight was controlling her, and the painful thoughts and feelings about her rape, helplessness, and victimization were still there. Losing weight did not get rid of them at all. Among trauma survivors, like Kelly, the binge-purge type is the most common form of anorexia.

Substance Abuse

Likewise, drug and alcohol abuse are more common among people with the binge-purge type of anorexia than they are among those with the restricting type. Substance abuse problems can complicate the treatment process. For instance, people with anorexia who abuse drugs and alcohol are likely to be less compliant with treatment recommendations and may need to participate in treatment for a longer period of time than people who do not abuse drugs. For this reason, unless the client's health is in grave danger, we generally recommend that the substance abuse be treated first.

Physical and Psychological Effects of Starvation

Conditions during World War II drew attention to the effects of semi-starvation on a person's physical and psychological well-being. During this time period, military blockades led to food shortages throughout Europe. Many prisoners of war were starved, and concentration camp victims were forced to survive on a daily food ration of bread and soup.

To learn more about the effects of semi-starvation and support famine relief efforts, University of Minnesota researchers designed an experiment in which volunteers who usually ate 3500 calories per day were limited to 1500 calories for six months (Franklin et al. 1948). While in a state of semi-starvation, the participants experienced physical symptoms that resemble symptoms of anorexia:

- Hair fell out in large clumps.

- Wounds were slower to heal.

- Muscles cramped and ached.

- Protruding bones made sitting painful.

- Pulse rate decreased.

- Cold temperatures became intolerable. Participants requested extremely hot foods and drinks.

- Sex drive diminished, and nocturnal ejaculation in men ceased.

- Time alone was preferred over social interaction.

- Irritability replaced a once calm demeanor.

- Chewing gum use (as many as forty packs per day) became a popular food substitute.

Apart from these physical and mood effects, investigators also noticed that the participants became preoccupied with food. For instance, they dreamt about food each night and talked about food throughout the day. Interestingly, some of these men never lost their obsession with food even after they were allowed to resume eating normally.

One of the important lessons of this study is that when food is restricted, we become preoccupied with it and food takes on a much larger role in our lives. In extreme cases, it takes over our lives. It is interesting that these effects occur regardless of whether food intake is restricted by force or by choice. The less people eat, the more they obsess about food. Does that sound like you? If so, you may be experiencing the physical and psychological effects of semi-starvation.

Let's review some of the physical effects that can result from intense dieting.

Physical Effects of Dieting Worksheet

To determine whether you experience any of the physical effects of intense dieting, please place a check mark next to the symptoms you experience:

_____ Irregular or absent periods/menstrual cycles

_____ Lanugo, a baby-fine "peach fuzz" hair growth, especially on the face

_____ Hair loss

_____ Weakness/fatigue

_____ Dizziness

_____ Irregular heartbeats

_____ Dry skin

_____ Frequent constipation

____ Edema (swelling/water retention)

____ Cold hands and/or feet

If you purge, you can experience these physical effects as well:

____ Frequent dental cavities

____ Sore, burning mouth or throat

____ Chest pain

____ Frequent heartburn

____ Enlarged/swollen salivary glands

If you put a check mark next to one or more of these symptoms, we recommend that you see a physician immediately. Even if you do not have any physical symptoms, we still recommend that, in addition to working through the program in this book, you also see a physician before we start treatment before your health deteriorates. The reason is that the medical and psychological aspects of anorexia both need to be treated.

Therefore, we urge you to contact your primary care doctor to monitor your physical condition. You should ask your doctor to perform blood work to assess your electrolyte levels, especially potassium, which affects your heart. If you feel that your health is in grave danger, go to your local hospital emergency room. Please refer to chapter 10 for more information on hospitalization and treatment options.

The Deadly Side of Anorexia

As you probably realize, anorexia can lead to several serious health consequences, such as heart problems, kidney problems, osteoporosis/bone weakening, and reproductive system damage that increases the risk of infertility and miscarriage. In severe cases, electrolyte imbalance and multiple organ failures can cause death.

The death of singer Karen Carpenter in 1983 drew the public's attention to anorexia's potentially deadly effects. Of the people with anorexia who are followed over a long period of time, as many as 20 percent (20 in 100) eventually die as a result of anorexia. Sadly, half of these deaths are suicides (Sullivan 1995). Approximately 5 percent (5 in 100 cases) die within ten years of developing the disorder. These numbers make anorexia the most deadly psychological disorder (Barlow and Durand 2003).

More important than these statistics are the real people and precious lives lost in the battle of trying to lose weight and be thin enough:

- Baby Hope, who was born prematurely to a recovering anorexic, died at three months of age. Her grieving mother prays that Jesus will hold Hope until they are reunited in heaven.

- The teen who dreamed of being a veterinarian. The dog she rescued from the pound still searches through the house for his lost companion.

- The straight-A college student whose roommate used to go into her room every night to check her pulse and breathing.

- The aspiring model whose fiancé proposed to her with a song he wrote. He planned to sing it at their wedding, but instead sang it at her funeral.

- The forty-three-year-old mother who died of heart failure one month before her son's high school graduation. She did not get to see him walk across the stage to receive his diploma.

The stolen dreams of these five women provide a compelling reminder. Today alone, approximately three people in the United States will die from anorexia, and they will leave behind unfulfilled lives. They will become statistics rather than the mother, spouse, or friend they wanted to be. So, yes, anorexia *can* kill you and take away your dreams.

Through ACT, you will learn to focus less on trying to control what is very costly to control—your weight and your painful thoughts and feelings about yourself—and start taking control of what is most important and maybe even fun to control: your life and what you want to do with it. In ACT you will learn that letting go of the struggle to be thin will free you and give you the energy you need to discover the value of your life. You will learn to take the steps to live fully on a daily basis.

The Causes of Anorexia

If you consider the significant and potentially deadly toll anorexia takes, the question that you may ask is *WHY?* What causes people to go to great extremes to reduce their weight? Why do people keep fighting with food, their weight, and the way their body looks? Why do they devote almost all their attention and energy to winning this fight—a fight that gets ever more difficult, costly, and all-consuming as time goes on? You may already have asked yourself similar questions.

In this section, we describe some of the issues that researchers have explored to find answers to these questions. Please note that it is unlikely that any one of these factors alone actually causes anorexia in an individual person. What is more likely is that multiple factors come together to create the condition we call anorexia. We can also tell you that the evidence from research studies is increasingly clear that social and cultural factors play a stronger role in the development of eating disorders than they do in just about any other psychological disorder.

Social-Cultural Influences

In an interview on the *Today Show*, England's Sarah Ferguson, Duchess of York, talked about going to a photo shoot for a magazine cover. She was apprehensive about posing because she had gained weight. At the shoot, she cried as she tried to squeeze her body into an outfit that was two sizes too small. In the end, she was impressed with how beautiful she appeared in the photos. Weeks after the shoot, her relief turned into disappointment. The magazine editor called and said the plan had changed: Fergie was "a bit too chubby," and would be replaced with a cover photo of Madonna.

This society bombards you with one disturbing message: *Be Thin*. If you look at a magazine cover, turn on your favorite TV show, or watch the Miss America Pageant, thinness is associated with success, beauty, and acceptance. If you want to be accepted and liked, you must be thin. In many cases, being thin is more important than being physically and mentally healthy.

Research has shown that the more women view fashion magazines, the worse they feel about their own bodies. Teens, especially, are vulnerable to feeling bad about themselves when they regularly read fashion magazines. One research study found that teenagers who read fifteen monthly issues of a fashion magazine felt worse about themselves than teenagers who had not regularly read such magazines (Stice, Spangler, and Agras 2001).

Most people don't realize that the thin ideal is nearly impossible to attain. The models on the magazine covers are airbrushed, cropped, and digitally enhanced. In a television interview, supermodel Cindy Crawford said that when women wish they could wake up in the morning looking like Cindy Crawford, they don't understand that this is her wish too. An eating disorder awareness flier states that only about ten women in the world are supermodels: The remaining *billions* are not.

Women in real life are not airbrushed, cropped, and digitally enhanced, and they do not come close to looking like the "ideal woman" presented by the media. To make things worse, when heavier people do appear in the media, they are often depicted as lazy, ugly, and unsuccessful.

In the 1980s, the teenage cast of the popular sitcom *The Facts of Life* gained weight as they developed into women. To have overweight main characters on prime time was publicly unacceptable. The girls were soon ridiculed as "The Fats of Life." Producers limited their access to food on the set and placed a scale in the rehearsal hall. Lisa Whelchel, who played Blair, was sent to fat farms, fitness experts, and hypnotists to shed the pounds. In a television interview, the actress said, "The normal facts of life were not allowed on *The Facts of Life*." If you are interested in reading the entire interview, you can find it on the Internet (see the exact address in the Resources section at the end of the book).

The pressure to be thin is magnified in women's athletics, especially in sports such as gymnastics, figure skating, and ballet. Joan Ryan (2000) documents several examples in her book, *Little Girls in Pretty Boxes*. In one case, a gymnastics official told Olympic gold medalist Mary Lou Retton that a half-point should be deducted for the fat hanging off her butt. A gymnastics judge recommended that eighty-five-pound Christy Henrich lose weight to boost her scores, while a coach dubbed her "The Pillsbury Dough Boy." Christy successfully lost weight, and she paid a high price for that success. First, she became too weak to make the 1992 Olympic Team. Then, in 1994, she died of medical complications from anorexia at the age of twenty-two, weighing only sixty-four pounds.

In general, Western culture values thinness, and we know that anorexia is more common in Western cultures than in less-developed nations. But anorexia is going global. In developed countries, such as Japan and Hong Kong, the occurrence of eating disorders is quickly approaching the numbers in the West (Barlow and Durand 2003). And researchers in Pakistan found that Pakistani women who had more exposure to Western culture were more likely to have an eating disorder than women with less exposure to Western culture (Suhail and Nisa 2002).

Lack of Control

Life is unpredictable, and many events happen that make us feel like we have no control. Someone you love may die. Your car might break down. You could be robbed. You may have a parent or spouse who is extremely controlling of you. One of the most frustrating aspects of life is that we cannot change the past, and we cannot control the behavior of other people. When the uncontrollable events of life begin to outweigh the controllable, the scale is tipped out of balance. That is how an eating disorder can develop.

Many people with anorexia people report that restrictive eating allows them to regain control in their life. The comments we hear from clients with anorexia reflect this need for control:

- Eating less gives me a sense of being in control.

- I am so proud of my self-control.

- It's all about control for me, and it always has been.

- I am using my looks to make myself feel in control of my life.

Take the example of Katie, a college student. Growing up, her mother never told Katie she was proud of her. Katie tried hard to please her mother, but nothing was ever good enough. If Katie cleaned the bathroom, mom was first to point out the spot on the sink she missed. Katie was able to identify that her mother's behavior was one thing she could not control, but what she *could* control was how much she ate. Becoming anorexic was Katie's way of regaining some of the control that her mother had stripped from her.

One of the goals of this ACT workbook is to help you recognize the problem of control and the traps you fall into when you use weight control to be in control of your life and what you think and feel. We will talk more about the issue of what you can and cannot control in chapter 4 because we believe it is crucial in dealing with anorexia.

At this point, we would simply like you to think of some examples in your life that are important and meaningful to you and that you have little or no control over. Then go to the worksheet below and write them down.

Things You'd Like to Control and Cannot Control

Use the space below to write down five examples in your life that are important and meaningful to you and that you have little or no control over.

1. _____

2. _____

3. _____

4. _____

5. _____

Family Interactions

In 1948, Elwood Stitzel wrote that poor parenting caused anorexia. He proposed that babies who were bottle-fed were unable to form an intimate association with their mother, and such improper feeding led a person to refuse food later in life. Modern research has discounted many of these early theories, which blamed families and especially mothers.

However, there is some evidence that people with anorexia, compared to those without anorexia, grew up in or still live in dysfunctional families. Specifically, the families of people with anorexia tend to be less supportive, overinvolved, and have difficulty resolving conflict. They are eager to maintain harmony by denying or ignoring problems. Studies have also shown that the families of women with anorexia are hard-driven and very concerned about success and appearances.

Research suggests that family problems are most common in cases in which the client has another psychological diagnosis in addition to anorexia (Mizes 1995). Although there is a relation between family distress and anorexia, it is difficult to determine which comes first. Do the family problems lead to anorexia? Or does anorexia disrupt the family functioning?

Genetics

Eating disorders run in families. If you have anorexia, you are more likely than someone without anorexia to have a close relative with an eating disorder. Twin studies are a common way to assess the role of genetics in the development of psychological disorders. There are two types of twins: identical and fraternal. Identical twins result when one fertilized egg divides into two separate babies, which means that identical twins share 100 percent of the same genes. Fraternal twins result when two separate eggs are fertilized. Fraternal twins only have 50 percent of their genes in common, which makes their genetic similarity equivalent to any set of siblings.

Typically, researchers compare the behavior of identical twins with the behavior of fraternal twins. If genes play a role in behavior, we would expect the behavior of identical twins to be more similar than the behavior of fraternal twins. This is the case with anorexia. Among people with anorexia who have a genetically identical twin, in 50 percent of the cases, both twins have anorexia. In contrast, only 7 percent of people with anorexia who have a fraternal (not genetically identical) twin share the disorder.

Likewise, the role of genetics in determining body shape is undeniable and strong (Brownell 1991). Your genes heavily influence the shape and size of your body. Of course, every healthy person can be physically fit, but for many individuals it is biologically impossible to come anywhere close to looking like fashion models and certain movie stars.

Just remember that you can't get any smaller than your bones will allow. If you inherited a heavy bone structure and "square" body shape from your parents, it is physically impossible to look like a ninety-five-pound, willowy fashion model. It is important for all of us, and particularly for people with eating disorders, to take note of and remember these basic genetic facts and not fight our biological makeup to the point of starvation.

What Caused Your Problem?

There are two short answers to this question that may frustrate you and give you some hope at the same time.

- Nobody really knows or will ever know for sure why *you* developed anorexia.

- It is not necessary for you to know what caused you to have anorexia. You can start rebuilding your life and moving in the direction you want to go without knowing why exactly you have a problem with anorexia.

Research studies have helped us gain a better understanding of the causes of anorexia, particularly the social-cultural ones. Yet it is impossible to apply data from studies involving thousands of people to your specific case. You may have some ideas of your own as to why you are experiencing problems with your eating and weight, and it may help to explore those ideas further. However, you may never find a satisfactory answer and you will never know for sure why *you* started having this problem.

The good news is that you do not really have to know what caused your eating problem to deal with it now and move on with your life. As we stated earlier, you cannot change the past, and no amount of insight into the causes of anorexia can take away or undo the events that might have led up to your developing this disorder. Even if you knew what happened *then*, you would still be stuck with the problem *now*.

So, in this workbook, we are going to focus on the present. We will focus on what you can do right now to take control of where you are going with your life today and in the future. You should be familiar with this approach to treatment from your experience with certain types of medical illnesses. For instance, when you have the flu, it does not matter who gave it to you or where you contracted it. The main concern is what you need to do *now* to heal yourself, be it bedrest or taking cold medicine. You do not have to understand every aspect of the flu problem as long as you are willing to do something to recover from it.

The ACT treatment approach that we will describe in Part II of this workbook will help you to simply acknowledge that you have a problem that you want to change. That is an important first step. If you are willing to try a new approach to dealing with your desire to be thin, we will teach you to accept what you cannot control and to commit to reclaiming your life. The ACT approach will refocus your energy on moving toward areas in your life that you value.

CHAPTER 2

An Anorexia Self-Test

In this chapter you will learn to assess how much you:

❋ Fear and avoid weight gain

❋ Feel you need to be thin to be accepted

❋ Try to control your weight in order to feel good

You probably have certain thoughts, worries, and concerns about eating, the way you look, and what other people think of you—and you probably feel strongly about some of these concerns. For this reason, it is important to assess how strongly you feel about these thoughts and concerns, what they mean to you, and how you respond to them. In this chapter you will assess in more detail some of your thoughts, worries, and attitudes about eating, the way you look, and what other people think of you.

In 1989, Scott Mizes and Robert Klesges developed the *Mizes Anorectic Cognitions Questionnaire*, also known as the MAC, to assess the extent to which people with anorexia experience specific thoughts and beliefs about eating and weight. Psychologists refer to thoughts and beliefs as *cognitions*. In 2000, Mizes and his colleagues revised the MAC.

Completing the MAC questionnaire is one way to assess how your personal beliefs about eating and weight compare to beliefs of other people with anorexia. The purpose of this questionnaire is not to establish whether you do or do not have anorexia but whether your thoughts, beliefs, and worries are similar to those of people who have been diagnosed with anorexia. This will clue you in to the severity of your problem.

Keep in mind that everyone is unique. That's why we recommend that you complete the MAC twice: now, and again after you complete this workbook. It's important to see how your personal beliefs and attitudes change *compared to where you are today*. Completing this questionnaire twice will tell you whether you react differently to your thoughts and feelings about your weight, body, and looks after reading this book and doing the exercises. An additional copy of this questionnaire is provided in Chapter 14 for you to complete when you finish the ACT program.

So here is what we would like you to do now. After reading each of the following statements, circle the number in the column that best reflects how much you agree or disagree with the statement. There are no right or wrong answers, so please don't think about your answers for very long. You should mark your answers quickly and then go on to the next statement.

Be sure to mark how you actually feel, not how you think you "should" feel. Try to avoid the "neither agree nor disagree" column, and only select "neither agree nor disagree" if you truly can't decide whether you agree or disagree.

		Strongly Disagree	Moderately Disagree	Neither Agree Nor Disagree	Moderately Agree	Strongly Agree
1.	I feel victorious over my hunger when I am able to refuse sweets.	1	2	3	4	5
2.	No matter how much I weigh, fats, sweets, breads, and cereals are bad food because they always turn into fat.	1	2	3	4	5
3.	No one likes fat people; therefore, I must remain thin to be liked by others.	1	2	3	4	5
4.	I am proud of myself when I control my urge to eat.	1	2	3	4	5
5.	When I eat desserts, I get fat. Therefore, I must never eat desserts so I won't be fat.	1	2	3	4	5
6.	How much I weigh has little to do with how popular I am.	5	4	3	2	1
7.	If I don't establish a daily routine, everything will be chaotic and I won't accomplish anything.	1	2	3	4	5
8.	My friends will like me regardless of how much I weigh.	5	4	3	2	1

9.	When I am overweight, I am not happy with my appearance. Gaining weight will take away the happiness I have with myself.	1	2	3	4	5
10.	People like you because of your personality, not whether you are overweight or not.	5	4	3	2	1
11.	When I eat something fattening, it doesn't bother me that I have temporarily let myself eat something I'm not supposed to.	5	4	3	2	1
12.	If I eat a sweet, it will be converted instantly into stomach fat.	1	2	3	4	5
13.	If my weight goes up, my self-esteem goes down.	1	2	3	4	5
14.	I can't enjoy anything because it will be taken away.	1	2	3	4	5
15.	It is more important to be a good person than it is to be thin.	5	4	3	2	1
16.	When I see someone who is overweight, I worry that I will be like him/her.	1	2	3	4	5
17.	All members of the opposite sex want a mate who has a perfect, thin body.	1	2	3	4	5
18.	Having a second serving of a high calorie food I really like doesn't make me feel guilty.	5	4	3	2	1
19.	If I can cut out all carbohydrates, I will never be fat.	1	2	3	4	5
20.	When I overeat, it has no effect on whether or not I feel like a strong person.	5	4	3	2	1

21.	Members of the opposite sex are more interested in "who" you are rather than whether or not you are thin.	5	4	3	2	1
22.	If I gain one pound, I'll go on and gain a hundred pounds, so I must keep precise control of my weight, food, and exercise.	1	2	3	4	5
23.	I rarely criticize myself if I have let my weight go up a few pounds.	5	4	3	2	1
24.	I try to attract members of the opposite sex through my personality rather than by being thin.	5	4	3	2	1

Your MAC Results

By following the directions below, you can interpret your MAC scores to assess how similar your beliefs and attitudes are to someone diagnosed with anorexia. The MAC items are divided into four scales:

- *Total Score*, which assesses your overall attitude about eating and weight

- *Weight Regulation*, which assesses how much you fear and avoid weight gain

- *Approval*, which assesses how much you feel the need to be thin to be accepted

- *Self-Control*, which assesses the extent to which you use weight control to feel good about yourself

Please be aware that everyone is unique and a low score on any of the scales does *not* mean you have no problem. It just means that your problems in that area are less severe *relative to the average person* who has been diagnosed with anorexia.

Total Score: Overall Attitude

Add up all the numbers you circled _____

Your total score reflects the overall level of anorexia beliefs that you experience. Research conducted by Mizes and colleagues (2000) has shown that clients diagnosed with anorexia have, on average, a total score of 75 or higher.

If your score is approximately 75, your beliefs about eating and weight are consistent with the average client with anorexia. If your score is greater than 75, it indicates that your beliefs are more extreme than those of the average client with anorexia. If your score is lower than 75, it means that your beliefs are less extreme than those of the average client with anorexia.

Accepting Your Thoughts

As you progress through this ACT workbook, you will learn to live with your thoughts. We will not challenge your thoughts or argue against them. The goal of ACT is not to get rid of any thoughts you experience. The goal of ACT is to help you experience these thoughts without needing to diet in response to them. In fact, the more you want to get rid of your thoughts, the more you have them. Instead of trying to replace your thoughts, we will encourage you to simply have them because you have them anyway, no matter what. Confused? That's okay. In the next chapter, we will give you a lot more information, examples, and exercises illustrating and applying the ACT view that you cannot win the battle against your thoughts. You'll also see how battling against your thoughts frequently backfires and makes things worse.

Weight Regulation Score

Add up the numbers you circled for the statements numbered:

2 ____   5 ____   7 ____   12 ____

14 ____   16 ____   19 ____   22 ____

Your Weight Regulation Score _____

The weight regulation scale assesses how much a person fears weight gain and engages in behaviors, like exercise and food restriction, to avoid weight gain. Research by Mizes and colleagues has shown that clients with anorexia have, on average, a weight regulation score of 23.

If your score is approximately 23, your weight gain fears and attempts to regulate your weight are similar to the fears and weight regulation behaviors of the average client with anorexia. A score greater than 23 indicates that your fears and regulation attempts are more extensive than the average client with anorexia, whereas a score of less than 23 indicates that your fears and regulation attempts are less extensive than the average client with anorexia.

One thing you may learn from this scale is how actively you respond to your thoughts about food and weight. Right now, your mind is saying, "You are fat," and you respond by doing something, like dieting, to prove your mind wrong. That seems like a natural way to respond. It might seem strange at this point to *not* respond to these disturbing thoughts. However, the ACT program will take you step-by-step through thought observation exercises—similar to meditation and mindfulness techniques used in yoga and Zen Buddhism. These exercises will teach you how to just observe your thoughts without acting on them.

As you progress through this ACT workbook, you will learn that letting go of the struggle with thoughts and feelings is possible and frees up time and energy to devote to activities that will enhance the quality of your life. You will move closer to reaching goals in your life that are not associated with your body, weight, and looks.

Approval Score

Add up the numbers you circled for the statements numbered:

3 ____   6 ____   8 ____   10 ____   15 ____   17 ____   21 ____   24 ____

Your Approval Score _____

The approval scale assesses how much you feel the need to be thin and attractive to be socially accepted. Research by Mizes and colleagues has shown that clients diagnosed with anorexia have, on average, an approval score of 20.

If your score is approximately 20, you place as much social value on thinness as the average anorexic client. A score greater than 20 suggests that you feel more social pressure to be thin than the average client with anorexia, whereas a score lower than 20 suggests that you feel less social pressure to be thin than the average client with anorexia.

One thing you may learn from your approval scale results is how much you value social acceptance. You may be someone who values having others view you in a positive way. That is who you are, and we are not going to attempt to change that. In fact, as you work through the valued directions chapters of this ACT workbook, we will encourage you to identify what you value about social approval and develop a plan to meet your need for social approval. We are particularly interested in how you see yourself in relationships—as a child, spouse, friend, parent, sibling, coworker. Being thin is only one way to feel accepted, and you may discover other ways to satisfy your desire for social acceptance.

Self-Control Score

Add up the numbers you circled for the statements numbered:

1 ____   4 ____   9 ____   11 ____   13 ____   18 ____   20 ____   23 ____

Your Self-Control Score _____

The self-control scale assesses how much feeling in control of eating is tied to how good you feel about yourself. Research by Mizes and colleagues has shown that clients diagnosed with anorexia have, on average, a self-control score of 32.

If your score is approximately 32, your need to control weight and eating as a basis for your self-esteem is similar to that of the average anorexic client. A score greater than 32 suggests that your need to be in control of your weight to feel good about yourself is greater than that of the average client with anorexia. On the other hand, a score lower than 32 suggests that feeling good about yourself is less closely tied to being in control of your weight than is the case with the average client with anorexia.

One thing you may learn from your self-control scale results is how much you need to feel in control. Ironically, people sometimes notice that the more they try to control their lives, the more out-of-control things get. Throughout this ACT workbook, especially in Chapter 4, we will explore the problem of control more in-depth.

Assessment Summary

Once again, the reason we asked you to assess these symptoms and put a number to them is to give you a baseline of where you stand now. We hope that you will learn to react differently to your thoughts, beliefs, and worries once you have completed the ACT workbook.

If your scores are lower after you complete the ACT workbook, this means you are not experiencing anorexic thoughts as often or intensely as you do now. You may also notice that you start believing them less. Such changes may bring you some relief. However, keep in mind that the main goal of ACT is not to change or reduce your thoughts, but to help you deal with them in a different way.

Our experience shows that when some people change their behavior and begin to pursue the most important things in life, their anorexic thoughts become less prominent. However, there are other people who still experience anorexic thoughts, although they may not buy into them so much anymore. Indeed, there is no guarantee your anorexic thoughts will ever disappear. Surely, if thoughts were that easy to get rid of, you would have been able to get rid of them by now.

Re-assessing your MAC results after you finish this workbook is one way to assess progress. However, the greatest gain you can make is to discover the strength that will propel you into action toward leading a valued life—with or without the thoughts and feelings that are associated with anorexia.

PART II

TREATING ANOREXIA WITH ACT:

Change What You Do, Not What You Think and Feel

CHAPTER 3

Accept—Choose—Take Action:
The Basics of Acceptance and Commitment Therapy

In this chapter you will learn:

* Everyone suffers—it's normal

* About the relationship between thoughts, feelings, and actions

* What it means to accept, choose, and take action

Until now, anorexia was your way of dealing with your painful feelings about yourself and your life. Acceptance and commitment therapy (ACT) teaches you that it is okay to have whatever thoughts and feelings your mind comes up with, and it gives you new tools for dealing with them. ACT involves a unique approach to understanding and dealing with suffering, and it encourages you to find and pursue what really matters to you. In a nutshell, ACT is about accepting yourself, choosing valued directions for your life, and committing to action that leads you in those directions.

Is Human Suffering Normal?

Have you recently watched afternoon TV talk shows? Have you listened to radio call-in shows with Dr. XYZ? Have you flipped through lifestyle or fashion magazines? If you have done any of these things, you will have come across all sorts of programs and suggestions to increase your self-esteem, improve your confidence, help you think more positively, and so on. There must be a reason why it pays to sell self-change advice on such a large scale day after day, year after year. Many people must be unhappy, insecure, pessimistic, and lacking in self-esteem. The fact that these TV and radio shows, books, and magazines have been bestsellers for many years also indicates that they don't work very well. If they did, fewer people would have to buy these products, and more people should already be much happier.

Yet in reality, more and more people are buying books and products to be happier, and still continue to feel miserable. Having tried out one of these "think-good-and-feel-good" programs, and failed, people move on to the next . . . and the next, feeling a little more frustrated and disappointed each time they fail. Why do people so frequently walk away from these programs as unhappy as they were before? Sometimes they feel even worse because they have added one more failure to their already long list of failures. Maybe people are just not doing it right? Maybe the programs would work if people only tried harder!?

Actually, we think it is difficult for people to "get it right" and succeed with these programs. The reason is that many of these programs are fundamentally flawed because they are based on two widely held beliefs that are myths and simply not true:

1. It is normal to be happy.

2. We need to think and feel better to be able to behave better.

You will recognize these myths when you read the following two statements that were posted by two women with anorexia on one of the many Internet chat rooms for people with anorexia.

- Becky, eighteen, college freshman, struggling with anorexia since age fourteen: *"Everyone seems to be happy. When I turn on MTV, all I see is boys and girls my age having a good time. Looking at my own miserable little life, I must be very different from all these other people my age because I neither look like them nor do I feel like them."*

- Amy, twenty-three, sales representative in a department store, struggling with anorexia since age sixteen: *"If I could only think and feel better, I would finally be able to do what I always wanted to do but never got to do because I don't seem to be able to overcome all my painful feelings."*

Myth #1: It Is Normal to Be Happy

If you look beyond the happy faces on magazine covers and really start talking to people about how they experience life, you will make a startling observation. Most people are suffering just like Becky, Amy, and yourself! In fact, the amount of suffering in our society seems overwhelming. Let's look at a few statistics (you can check these numbers in any textbook on "abnormal" psychology, e.g. Barlow and Durand 2003). Over 20 million people in the United States are alcoholics, more than 30,000 people in the U.S. successfully commit suicide each year, an estimated 600,000 attempt suicide, and millions think about suicide each year. A large national survey (Kessler et al. 1995) found that more than 29 percent of adults between the ages of fifteen and fifty-nine had suffered from at least one diagnosable psychological disorder in the previous year. The same survey found that almost 50 percent of the U.S. population suffers from a diagnosable psychological disorder at one point in their lives.

As staggering as these numbers are, they actually *under*estimate the degree of suffering, because they only count "diagnosable" disorders, which are the textbook cases in which a person meets all the diagnostic criteria that psychologists and psychiatrists have put together. The numbers would be even higher if we also included people who meet some but not all of the diagnostic criteria for a disorder. This so-called "subclinical" suffering is painful and miserable nonetheless. One of our colleagues (Hayes 2003, personal communication) put it this way: "Look around you next time you go to a store. Really, really look at the people in there. Watch how they carry themselves. What you will see is an incredible amount of pain, suffering, and dignity. I sometimes find myself tearing up just walking around town. When I look around, the amount of pain (and courage) in human beings is simply staggering."

We could go on with more statistics and facts, but we think you get the general picture and message: Psychological suffering is pervasive, much more pervasive than most people would ever suspect.

It's Okay for You to Suffer

We understand it if you find these statistics on suffering depressing. Yet you may also find something very liberating in these numbers. If so many people are suffering, and if suffering is simply the norm, then maybe it is okay for you to suffer, too. Perhaps your suffering is not that abnormal after all. At this point, we can imagine you sitting very uncomfortably in your chair and perhaps even yelling out, *"But I don't want to suffer! I want this book to help me stop suffering! Suffering sucks—that's why I am reading this book, to end the suffering. I've had enough of it."*

We understand your frustration and feel it, too! This is not just a hollow, patronizing phrase. We really do feel it because we suffer, too. Just like you, we are human beings, and therefore we suffer. Of course, the exact nature of your suffering and our suffering is likely to differ, but there is probably more overlap and shared experience than you might think. We truly share this aspect of our existence with every other human being. Most of us prefer to be happy rather than sad. Most of us prefer to experience joy rather than despair and failure. And yet we all do suffer.

The Pursuit of Happiness

The Declaration of Independence mentions each person's right to "the pursuit of happiness." Most people think that amounts to a right to *be* happy, when in fact all that the Declaration refers to is your right to *pursue* happiness. So there is definitely no guaranteed right to be happy. People only pursue things they don't have. So the pursuit of happiness is a constant reminder that you are not happy. Feeling happy is a goal, and people get upset when they don't have it (Hayes 2003, personal communication). When they do occasionally feel happy, they quickly start to worry about losing this elusive state. An alternative to trying to feel happy is to engage in activities and do things that express love and compassion to yourself and others.

Perhaps happiness is somewhat overrated anyway. ACT creator Steven Hayes shared with us some experience from working with adults in workshops. When he asked them what they were looking for as little kids, the adults would say things like acceptance, love, caring, being noticed, safety, and respect. "Happiness" was not mentioned once as something that they wanted as children. Perhaps if we have these other things, sometimes we are happy, sometimes we are sad, and we are always alive. When we look at the relationship between suffering and happiness, a number of questions come to mind, some of which we will explore in subsequent chapters. Is there perhaps a way that we can suffer *and* do happy and valued things at the same time? Could we suffer and do joyful things at the same time? You may think suffering and joy are contradictory. You either experience suffering or you experience joy—surely, it's impossible to experience both at the same time?

As odd as it may sound, there are ways for us to suffer *and* also find fulfillment in what we do with our lives—all at the same time. This is what the ACT approach is all about: Accept and have what there is to have (suffering, joy, and all) while also staying committed to doing what needs to be done to live a fulfilled rich life according to your chosen values. You can choose to do things you enjoy and value regardless of what it is that you feel.

Why Do I Suffer?

This is a tough question and it may help to rephrase the question slightly and ask yourself: When do I suffer and what makes me suffer? Answers to these questions might help you move in a new direction that gets you "un-stuck" and keeps you from reentering the same old dead-end streets you've walked in the past.

We suffer when bad things happen to us. You get hit by a car, you get a disease, you lose a loved one. This type of suffering happens to all of us and is simply a function of living. In ACT we call this type of suffering *clean discomfort*. Life serves up these events, and it is normal and appropriate when we respond to such events with sadness and behave in a way that attempts to remedy the situation.

We suffer when we do not accept our reactions to painful events. When we do not accept our feelings of sadness and uncertainty and struggle to get rid of them, clean discomfort (sadness) turns into *dirty discomfort*. Dirty discomfort occurs when we don't want to be sad or hurt, and we do things to escape from experiencing sadness or pain. This leads us to become sad over being sad and fearful over having fear. We start doing things to avoid our feelings. We have found that dieting can be a way to avoid emotional pain. In chapter 4, we will therefore discuss in more detail how dieting is one way people can avoid dealing with their feelings.

The Dark Side of Language

Did you know that babies and animals don't starve themselves? Why is that, you may wonder? We suspect the answer is that they do not have language to constantly compare and evaluate themselves, situations, events, and other people. Language has given humans extraordinary capabilities—an "evolutionary edge" ability to respond to and adapt to all sorts of changes and conditions. For instance, you can learn and survive without having direct experiences—you can just read or talk to other people. You can plan your actions years in advance. So what is it about this powerful, positive language force that also puts us at risk for developing anorexia and certain other psychological conditions?

Just like in *Star Wars*, there is a dark side to the language force. Language allows us to bring things to life in our mind as dangerous or desirable even though they are actually not present in our immediate environment. We can make things happen with our mind and in our mind as if they were the real thing. And then we respond to these words and thoughts, with feeling and sometimes with real action, as if they are real! To illustrate this point, let us look at the following four examples and exercises:

Example: Nobody Will Ever Love Me

Imagine a lonely woman who tells her friend that she doesn't believe anyone will ever love her again. Her friend says to her, "Don't think like that. Surely you'll find love again in the future." Why is it that her friend tries so hard to change the way the woman thinks and feels? The underlying assumption is that the woman must feel courageous to be courageous, and that she must believe love is possible in order to behave in a loving manner. If we accept this assumption, we will set out to fight not only objectively dangerous or threatening events, but also our own reactions to those circumstances. In other words, we will not only try to fight events that can truly harm us, we will also fight our feelings and thoughts about these events (Wilson and Murrell 2003).

Example: Thinking Creates Feelings

We would like you to do a little exercise now so that you can actually experience how thinking creates feelings. Please think about the death of the person who you love most in the world. Just think about it for a moment. . . . Did you notice some reluctance in you when you read the instruction? You probably didn't want to follow that instruction and wished we had asked you to do something else. Why would you cringe at such a request? In addition to avoiding real death and danger (which keeps us alive and our species from extinction), people often avoid the very thought of death, as if the thought of death and actual death were one and the same (Wilson and Murrell 2003). We can create feelings by simply thinking certain thoughts and imagining certain events and activities. This capacity to create feelings may be helpful in some instances, it may be benign or not harmful in others, and it can be downright destructive in other instances.

Example: You Are Not What You Think

Sit back for a moment and see what happens when you think or say to yourself, "I am fat and worthless." Go ahead and say it: "I am fat and worthless." How do you feel when you say that or think that? Are fat and worthless just two simple words? Is the thought just a simple thought? If you're like most people, the thought of being fat probably makes you feel uncomfortable, perhaps even very uncomfortable. Why is that? After all, fat and worthless are just words, and thinking, "I am fat and worthless," is just another thought. This is a good example of how the dark force of language exerts its power. By thinking or saying to yourself, "*I am* fat and worthless," you connect worthlessness with fatness, and both worthlessness and fatness to you as a person. Fatness, worthlessness, and you become one and the same. You are fatness. Thinking and saying it in this way brings the feeling of worthlessness alive in you. You react to the words or the thought as if you are the embodiment of fatness and worthlessness—you are it.

Example: Getting Off Your But

Have you ever heard yourself say something like, "I could go out with my friends, but I am self-conscious about my body"? What you are saying here is that going out cannot occur along with feelings of self-consciousness. By saying *but* after the first part of the sentence, you undo what you said—you make it go away. This is actually what the word "but" literally means. "But" derives from the words "be out" and undoes or discounts everything that precedes it (Hayes et al. 1999). So if you say, "I could go out with my friends, but I am self-conscious about my body," you will not go out. You stay home. The reason is that "but" takes the "could" away. Unfortunately we use the word "but" many times every day and it restricts our lives in unnecessary and unfortunate ways. It reduces your options.

Now imagine what would happen if you simply replaced the word "but" with "and." "I could go out with my friends *and* I am self-conscious about my body." This little change has a dramatic impact on what might happen next. If you put it that way, you could actually go out *and* be self-conscious all at the same time. It would allow you to go out. It would also be a more correct and honest statement because you might indeed feel anxious about your body in the context of going out with your friends. Imagine what would happen if you started to say "and" instead of "but" more often. Imagine how much more space you would have in your life. How many more opportunities would you gain to do things? How much space would open up for you? Getting off your but(t)s could be one of the most empowering things you've ever done.

Kathy Got Off Her But(t). Kathy was a nineteen-year-old college sophomore with anorexia. She was feeling lonely and was very self-conscious about her weight and looks. Kathy used to tell herself (and us), "I can't go out to parties with my friends because I'm fat," and, "I'd like to go out, but I feel so bad about the way I look." Kathy acted on her but and did not go to the party. She was waiting to lose weight to look better so that she would feel better about herself. *Then* she was going to start going out. What Kathy did not realize was how much her buts perpetuated her discomfort and suffering. It literally kept her stuck at home away from the opportunity to have fun with her friends. This type of discomfort was not of the clean type; it was not served up by life's inevitable mishaps. This discomfort occurred as a result of the way language can sabotage a person's potential to live a valued life. When we spoke with Kathy about her buts, she gradually started to replace her buts with ands. It was a slow process and she frequently fell back to her old but. When she did use "and," she found it helpful because it pointed her in the direction of what could happen. She could go out *and* be somewhat uncomfortable *and* have some fun. It was more honest and in line with what she really felt, and it helped her go out and start doing things that were in line with her values.

Suffering from Avoiding Our Experiences

When animals try to avoid pain, they avoid the situations and events in which pain actually occurs. They avoid real events, situations, or objects. We humans do that, too. This kind of avoidance is very useful and adaptive because it literally keeps us out of trouble, safe and alive. When we cannot avoid such events, we may indeed suffer or even die.

Human suffering does not stop there, however. Humans create another level of suffering by avoiding the painful thoughts and feelings that are associated with such events. This level of suffering can only occur because we have language. When a thug attacks you with a knife, you have every reason to experience anxiety and act on it. For instance, you may try to escape, or if that is not possible, you may try to fend off the perpetrator. This is appropriate because it is a response to a real event that endangers you. Yet when you think about a sad event of the past or a potentially sad event in the future, you may feel as sad now as if you were experiencing the real event, when in fact your current feeling of sadness is nothing but a feeling or a thought. Yet you may try to avoid sadness and other feelings as if they were the real event. The consequences of trying to run away from what you feel can be costly in terms of restricting your living space. It can seriously debilitate your life.

The question, then is, why do we do that? Why do we avoid feelings and thoughts as if they are the enemy? Again, it has to do with language. The learning of such avoidance starts very early and is pervasive. Our culture (parents, schools, the media) teaches us that some thoughts and feelings (happiness, pride) are good and that other thoughts and feelings (sadness, anger) are bad and should be eliminated or at least minimized. From the time we are little children, we are taught that we can and should control what we think and how we feel, particularly those "negative" thoughts and feelings. The little boy who cries on the playground is told, "Pull yourself together. Don't be a baby." Just think of how many times you have heard parents or teachers saying things like, "Don't worry. There is no reason to be afraid and cry."

We talked with twenty-year-old Karen about the issue of how people learn to get rid of unwanted thoughts and feelings. She shared some vivid childhood memories with us. In these stories she described how her parents taught her to control her fears and occasional sadness. She also realized that this had become a way of life for her as a young adult:

> I remember when I was a little girl I would sometimes lie in bed at night and just feel bad and cry. My parents could not stand hearing me cry because it probably made them feel bad when I felt bad. So they would come and talk to me and tell me not to cry because there was nothing to be afraid of or sad about. When I told them I sometimes felt lonely in bed, they told me every time I felt that way I should just think about something nice and fun—then I would feel different, too. I tried hard to do so in order to not feel the way I did. It didn't really work but I guess it taught me that feeling bad and crying is bad and that I needed to do something so I wouldn't feel that way anymore. I seem to be doing that to this day. For instance, I can't stand the way I look, and I feel disgusted. I just want to have a different type of body so that I can feel better about myself.

This kind of learning sets you up to avoid experiencing your thoughts and feelings. As a consequence, you try hard to control, reduce, or eliminate certain thoughts and feelings because you "just can't stand them." In the next chapter, you will learn more about how such control efforts set you up to perpetuate your struggle with uncontrollable thoughts and emotions and how ACT may help you to give up this struggle and focus on what you can control and change.

Myth 2: Think Good → Feel Good → Act Good

If we have the idea that we feel bad because we think bad thoughts, the logical consequence is to change those bad thoughts and replace them with more positive ones so that we may feel better. Then, if we think and feel better, we will behave more effectively. These ideas are widespread in our society. Even in psychological science there is an approach to therapy that operates on the same basic assumption: people need to challenge or replace negative thoughts with more positive thoughts.

There is indeed research evidence showing that if we think more positively, we are likely to feel better and act more effectively. So we aren't arguing with the idea that thinking positive thoughts is generally helpful and may lead to more effective behavior and better outcomes. We are, however, challenging the idea that we *must* think positively to act in ways that move us in the direction of our own personal values. We *can* act before we think and feel good.

The case of Mr. Robert shows us that challenging and attempting to replace "faulty thinking" may only perpetuate the struggle with thoughts (and feelings). Author Georg learned this lesson the hard way as an inexperienced psychology student completing his first clinical practicum in a locked psychiatric ward for people with serious psychological problems.

Arguing with Thoughts Prolongs the Struggle

Mr. Robert was a sixty-eight-year-old man who spent most of his days walking up and down the psychiatric ward with a very sad face, his eyes looking down, and his body hunched forward. He literally seemed to carry the burden of the world on his two frail shoulders. When I asked him why he was so sad, the man told me that he was responsible for bankrupting the company he had worked for and ruining the livelihood of all its twenty-four employees. As a result of his actions, he was personally liable for the loss of $8 million. It didn't seem plausible that this kind and gentle man could have ruined the entire company. I asked him to explain how exactly he had managed to ruin an entire company and noticed some inconsistencies in his story. When I mentioned them to Mr. Robert, he added some information to make the story more consistent.

The next day I saw him again carrying his heavy burden and asked him how he felt. He looked at me with a grave expression on his face and replied, "Wouldn't you feel guilty if you had ruined so many lives and were in debt for $9 million?" When asked why he would now owe $9 million ($1 million more than yesterday), he replied he hadn't explained everything before. I then specifically focused on aspects of his story that could shift some of the blame away from him, hoping that this would help him feel less guilty and sad. During this conversation Mr. Robert became increasingly upset. The next day his back seemed even further hunched down and his face had an expression of utter despair. He had added new, elaborate twists to his story that would put all the blame squarely onto him. In fact, Mr. Robert had used all of my arguments to make his story more consistent with his deeply held conviction: *I am guilty of terrible things and deserve to be punished.*

Fortunately for Mr. Robert, my supervisor finally caught on to what had been going on in the corridor for the past three days and put an end to my well-meaning but obviously failing "therapy." He explained that you cannot simply change a patient's web of delusions by pointing out logical or factual inconsistencies. In fact, doing so makes things worse because patients will incorporate your arguments into their delusions to make their story consistent again. As a result, the web of delusions becomes more elaborate, intricate, and harder to change. Due to my lack of experience, I incorrectly assumed that if I could only demonstrate to Mr. Ro.bert the fallacies in his thinking, he would feel less guilty, sad, and worried. Unfortunately, the exact opposite happened. Challenging his thoughts and attempting to change them only exacerbated and perpetuated the man's struggle with his twisted thoughts.

Must You Feel and Think Better to Act Better?

In the early days of behavior therapy about fifty years ago, therapists typically focused on how they could help their clients change their behavior. They didn't worry too much about what clients thought and felt. Some therapists considered that a flaw. So about thirty years ago, *cognitive* behavioral therapists attempted to change both behavior and thinking to help their patients overcome their problems.

We were trained to do that with our clients, too. Yet we often felt a bit hypocritical when we were trying to change a client's thinking because this strategy did not work very well personally. When Georg felt insecure about giving a speech, it didn't seem to help much when he tried to get rid of that feeling by changing his doubting, negative thoughts. For instance, he tried to recall evidence that he had mastered such situations before and then asked himself why it should be different this time. There was really no justification for feeling insecure—the evidence suggested that he should do just fine. This evidentiary strategy did not really seem to help much. The only thing that seemed to make a *real* difference was actually going out there and giving the speech (and taking the feelings of insecurity and anxiety along). Then, *after* doing what needed to be done, he actually felt more confident.

So what happened here? Behaving in a confident way led to the feeling of confidence. The feeling of confidence came after behaving in a confident way while feelings of insecurity and fear of failure were still present. In contrast, many people try to feel confident first, before they act. They argue that they must *feel good first* and *then* they can act—just like our patient Kathy whom we introduced earlier: "When I feel confident about the way I look, I can go out to a party." The problem is that if you adopt this strategy you may never get to the party because you may never feel confident *beforehand*!

If you think that only individuals with problems do that, take a look at attitude change strategies commonly employed by companies. They work on the same assumption as Kathy used to. For instance, advertisers spend millions of dollars every year to change people's attitudes with the hope that attitude change will lead to subsequent behavior change. Likewise, public health agencies mount programs to change teenagers' attitudes to prevent them from taking up smoking or to get them to quit smoking. Yet many research studies have demonstrated that this strategy is not very effective. Instead, it is more effective to attempt to change behavior first and let thoughts and feelings take care of themselves. You see, once behavior changes, thoughts and feelings often change *as a consequence*.

What this means is that you need not change your thoughts or feelings first before you can give new direction to your life by changing what you do. You can act before you "get things right in your head." Using the ACT approach, it is unnecessary to straighten out, change, or get rid of unwanted thoughts and images in your mind before you can improve your life—heck, you may never get them right anyway (whatever *right* may mean)! In the next chapter you will learn that it is not only unnecessary, it actually causes problems when you desperately try to control or change your thoughts and feelings, particularly those about yourself.

If you hang on to the old idea that you must first change your thoughts and feelings before you act, then you are stuck. It just won't work. In the next chapter we will do some exercises to let you experience that this control struggle is hopeless. Please note what we are saying here: your *struggle* is hopeless. We are not saying that *you* are hopeless. Also please know that you are not alone in this struggle. We are *all* in it, and we all help keep it alive by participating in it. It is part of the social system we live in, and our language is not helping us here either.

Is there a way out? We think so. The ACT approach encourages you to go with and follow your experience rather than what your mind tells you when it plays its mind games on you. We no longer want you to let your mind trick you and keep you stuck where you are.

The ACT Approach to Treating Anorexia

In ACT we encourage you to end your struggles with your thoughts and feelings. In this workbook we will neither challenge nor help you argue with your thoughts about your weight and body. Our goal is not to get rid of or change the thoughts you experience. Our goal is to help you experience these thoughts without dieting in response to them, without agreeing with them, without arguing with them. In ACT, we encourage you to simply have your thoughts because you have them anyway, no matter what. Confused? Let's do an exercise.

Tug-of-War of the Mind

If you are a little confused what all this talk about "arguing with your thoughts" and not responding to them means, think of a tug-of-war. How can a tug-of-war end? How can it be resolved? Most people think there are only two possible endings: either the team on the right side wins by pulling harder than the team on the left side *or* the left team wins by pulling harder than the right team. Either way, the teams will fight until one of them has overpowered or worn out the other. They will spend all their energy fighting each other. It seems they are doomed to fight until the end, right?

There is another way to end the tug-of-war that people typically do not think of because they are busy fighting the other team. This solution may surprise you too: *one of the teams could simply drop the rope!* Just imagine, what would happen if the team on the right simply refused to fight anymore and just dropped the rope? The fight would stop in an instant. The team members would still all be there *and* the fight would be over.

You may wonder, "What does all that have to do with my thoughts and feelings?" We will give you a hint: imagine the team members on the left are all your thoughts about anorexia, being too fat, gaining weight, your looks, etc. Now imagine that the team members on the right are all the other thoughts that you sometimes try to think to calm yourself or make yourself feel better ("Maybe I am not *that* bad looking after all," "Even if I don't like myself, maybe someone else will"). Have you noticed what's happening with the thoughts that you're fighting because you don't want them? Doesn't it feel like the left team ultimately always comes back no matter how hard the right team fights back?

Now imagine that one day you would come along to the game site, pick up the rope, and then when the other team starts pulling, you do something very different, something that changes the game dramatically: you simply drop the rope . . . you just let it go. . . . Imagine that you stop trying to decide which thought is right and which one is wrong . . . which thought to have or not to have. What would happen if you stopped being on one side of the rope *or* the other? After all, both teams are yours—they are *both* your thoughts! We understand that you may prefer if one team could win once and for all. But how many months and years are you willing to go on fighting the other team? How much energy are you going to devote to winning this game every day, every month, every year, again and again? Imagine what would happen if instead of fighting you just got out of playing the mind game altogether . . . if you ended the tug-of-war of the mind? What would that be like? What would it feel like? What could you do instead with all your time and energy that is no longer spent on winning the tug-of-war?

Accept—Choose—Take Action

One of the best ways to understand the basics of ACT is to use the three letters to remember what ACT is ultimately all about: Accept—Choose—Take action. Remember, these are just the basic principles of ACT—the specific techniques will be covered in the next few chapters.

Accept

This is the first step in ACT. It involves accepting thoughts and feelings about yourself that are essentially not controllable. The idea is to accept what you already have anyway and end the struggle with unwanted thoughts and feelings by not attempting to eliminate or change them, by not acting upon them and ultimately letting them go.

Choose

The second step is about choosing a direction for your life. It involves identifying what you value in life and what you want your life to stand for. It is about helping you to discover what is truly important to you—what you value—and then making a choice. What kind of daughter, sister, student, friend do you want to be? What types of activities are meaningful to you? It is about choosing to go forward in directions that are uniquely yours and accepting what is inside you and what comes with you and accompanies you along the way.

Take Action

The third aspect involves taking steps toward realizing your valued life goals. It is about making a commitment to action and changing what you can change. This last important stage of ACT involves learning to behave in a way that moves you forward in the direction of your chosen values. In this stage of ACT, you begin to see that there is a difference between you as a person and the thoughts and feeling you have about yourself. Life itself is asking you this question: are you willing to contact and stay in touch with those experiences, fully and without avoiding or trying to escape from them? If the answer is "no," you get smaller. If the answer is "yes," you get bigger and behavior change will become your focus (Hayes, Masuda, and DeMey 2003).

You may feel intimidated by these three big, bold steps. In fact, you may be quite scared. You may say, this is too big—I can't do this. If you do feel this way or have other similar thoughts and feelings, that's fine. Remember our little exercise, "I am having the thought that. . . ."? You cannot and need not control the occurrence or disappearance of such thoughts and feelings. What you can control is what you do with your eye muscles and your hand muscles. So just keep the book in your hands, use your eye muscles to keep on reading, *and* let the thoughts be what they are and do what they do. Like all other thoughts and feelings, it is okay if they come, it is okay if they stay, and it is also okay if they go.

Let us close this chapter with a final remark on suffering. Although we have told you numerous times that suffering is normal, ACT does seek to reduce suffering. It seeks to do so by increasing your vitality and ability to do what you want to do with your life. The goal is to help you live a life that moves you in directions that you have chosen. ACT does not seek to reduce pain or to produce a particular positive feeling. You may feel less pain and more enjoyment, but that's not a goal. Suffering comes from a root word that means carrying or bearing (the same root as the word "ferry"). It's like we are carrying our pain in a sack, waiting for something to do with it (Hayes, 2003, personal communication). It is the "what you do with it" part that ACT targets and that we target in this workbook.

CHAPTER 4

When Control Gets
Out of Control

In this chapter you will learn to:

❋ Explore the benefits of anorexia

❋ Evaluate the need for control in your life

❋ View control as a problem, not a solution

❋ Prepare to let go of your struggle

It might seem that when treating clients with anorexia, the most logical approach would be to first discuss all of the reasons why anorexia is "bad": you could die, you could become infertile, people tease you about being so thin, and so on. However, we're sure you have heard it all before. Most people with anorexia know the dangers. You can probably recall countless situations when other people nagged at you, "Why are you doing this to yourself. Don't you know you can die?" You've heard the message a thousand times. There is no need for us to add to the chorus of voices telling you why you should start eating more.

You Can't Just Snap Out of It

Obviously, reminding you of the negatives has not worked; otherwise, you would be "cured" by now. It is very important for us not to make the same mistake that other well-intentioned people in your life have made. We don't assume that you can just snap out of it and start eating more. It is hard for some people to understand that it's not that simple.

Take the case of Stacey, who dropped enough weight to reach her personal goal weight. After she reached that goal, she still could not stop dieting and wanted to lose "just a few more pounds." One night, her boyfriend began to shake her and yell, "Why can't you just eat like a normal person!" As you can imagine, this comment was not helpful and only made Stacey diet more, not less.

People with anorexia are neither stupid nor crazy, and they usually don't have a death wish. They diet because weight control plays an important role in their life. There are reasons why someone with anorexia diets, and you have a reason why you have been dieting too. You may very well want to change. At the same time, the thought of life without dieting may be very scary for you.

In this chapter, we will discuss all the reasons why you may continue to diet. We believe it is much more important to talk about the pros—the benefits of anorexia—than the cons or the dangers of anorexia. You may wonder what those benefits are and why it isn't the therapist's job to convince the client that dieting is bad, and the client must stop now. To focus on the benefits of anorexia may seem like heading in the wrong direction, almost like giving someone who wants to commit suicide a rope to hang himself. Yet you will discover that it's not so odd to talk about the benefits after all.

The Benefits of Anorexia

Researchers Cockell, Geller, and Linden (2002) assessed hundreds of women with anorexia to see what role dieting played in their lives. Here is a sample of the benefits women reported. When you read these reports, think about what dieting does for you, what it means to you, and why you are doing it. Do you recognize any of these arguments for dieting and losing weight?

- Anorexia is my way of being more perfect (or at least less imperfect).

- Anorexia makes me feel unique and special.

- Anorexia gives me a sense of self-control.

- Low weight makes me feel more confident.

- Add your own: _____

In addition to these reasons, Cockell and her colleagues also made another really important observation. She noticed that many women diet as a way to cope with stressful situations and bad feelings about themselves. Do you diet to cope with pain? In the research study, the women reported:

- Anorexia is my way of avoiding serious problems.

- Anorexia is my way of escaping from thoughts about myself I don't like.

- Anorexia distracts me from noticing my painful emotions.

- Anorexia allows me to avoid my fears about sex and sexuality.

- Add your own: _____

As you read carefully through the above list, you may recognize some of the reasons why you continue to diet. You aren't going to just snap out of it! When it comes to intense dieting, you can't live with it (you could literally die), and it seems that you can't live without it either. You may find yourself suffering because you are being torn in two different directions.

Anorexia: Can't Live With It, Can't Live Without It

Your resulting confusion and pain are very normal. Here are some typical statements of women who can't let go of the role anorexia plays in their life:

- Sarah, office clerk, nineteen years old: *With all the problems I have, if I can't create the life I want, I will make my body look the way I want. I know it's stupid, but I don't know what else to do.*

- Gwen, mother, twenty-eight years old: *My family always notices when I gain an extra pound or two. I stop eating because I feel embarrassed. I have tried to break this cycle, but I am totally caught up in this. I am stuck. I hate it.*

- Natalie, beautician, twenty-two years old: *When I go to bed, I think about what I ate that day, and I feel a sense of achievement if I met my 500-calorie limit. The problem is, that feeling of power and pride is gone when I wake up, and I have to start over the next day to once again achieve that feeling.*

- Dolly, high school soccer player, sixteen years old: *My parents fought constantly when they first separated, and I felt so helpless. I didn't know what to do, so I stopped eating. At first, dieting made me feel better, but now I have no control over my eating. If I don't diet, I feel like I might become a great ball of fat.*

- Susan, college student, twenty-four years old: *This whole weight thing is all about competing—it has always been that way for me. I could never keep up with my girl-friends. They always had better grades, better boyfriends, got into better colleges, made more money. I constantly felt bad about that and about myself because they always seemed so far ahead of me in regard to everything that was important to me. Dieting has been my way of keeping up with them. When it comes to losing pounds, they can't beat me. I'm the best—that is where I am the champion.*

Your Reasons for Dieting

Please read the statements by Sarah, Gwen, Natalie, Dolly, and Susan again. Do any of these statements fit *your* life? Write down how and what you feel as you read these statements. What does dieting do for you?

_____

_____

_____

If you read the statements from Sarah, Gwen, Natalie, Dolly, and Susan more carefully, you will discover that they actually share two common themes:

1. First, they reflect the use of dieting and weight to gain or regain control over an aspect of the woman's life. In these examples, dieting is a way to gain a sense of empowerment and achievement, as well as a way to cope with difficult life events, such as a divorce in the family.

2. The second theme is even more striking and important. The statements all show that dieting fails to lead to lasting, long-term control over thoughts and feelings that the women do not like and want to get rid of. It's like you're in a race in which the finish line keeps moving back. At some point, you realize there is no real finish line.

Do any of these themes apply to your situation? You may realize that you are in a similar situation, although the particular circumstances may be different. On the one hand, dieting and losing weight may be the only way you know of to cope with an out-of-control situation. It may be the only way for you to feel successful in an unfair world. Or it may be the only way to help you feel good about yourself. On the other hand, dieting is causing you to suffer. You may feel physically weak and unable to do things you want to do.

You may start out feeling good when you successfully control how much you eat and lose weight. As time goes on, you may find that it either does not work or does not take long before you start feeling worse again. Just as Natalie described on the previous page, you're stuck having to lose more weight to feel good again. You are caught in a vicious circle. That is what we mean in ACT when we say, "Control is the problem, not the solution."

Digging Yourself Into a Hole

Your situation reminds us of a story originally told by the founders of ACT, Steven Hayes and his colleagues (1999):

The Story of the Child in the Hole

Imagine a happy child running through a wide-open field. That is how life is supposed to be: fresh and carefree. Try to image this scene vividly. Now, in a sad twist of fate, imagine the child running through the field and falling into a hole. The perfect life is now imperfect. The child struggles and struggles to climb out of the hole, but there is no escape. If climbing won't work, there must be another way out. She thinks to herself, "Maybe digging is the way out." So, the child squats down on her hands and knees and starts to dig. She digs and digs and digs . . . and keeps on digging.

Yet after all this digging, where is the child? She looks around, and she is still in the hole. So she tries to dig much harder and faster, thinking to herself, "Maybe it will work if I just work harder at it." After a while, she stops and looks around again. And where does she find herself? She is even deeper in the hole. All this effort. All this work. And what is the result? The hole has only gotten deeper and wider. It feels scary being trapped deeper in the hole.

Is this your experience? Clearly, the problem is not lack of effort. The child is giving all she has to dig herself out, but the effort is not paying off. In fact, the effort is only creating a bigger problem. The harder she digs, the deeper the hole gets. Her situation has actually become worse because now the hole is even deeper than when she started.

For you, anorexia may be a way of digging yourself out of a hole that life has let you fall into. You may notice that dieting only digs you deeper into your hole. Think about a hole you have fallen into. That hole can be a number of different situations: a bad relationship, a bad grade, a nasty comment someone made about your appearance, or any other difficult situation. You can refer back to your personal examples of uncontrollable situations you listed in chapter 1. Has dieting made your situation any better? Has dieting worked for you? Has dieting harder worked for you?

There has got to be a more useful way than digging yourself ever deeper into the hole. So in this workbook we will not offer you a better way of digging because better digging is still digging and will make your hole bigger and deeper. Instead, in chapters 5 and 6 we will teach you to let go of the digging. You will learn to free your hands to do other things with them than digging.

Your Coping Style: A Questionnaire

Complete the following questionnaire to see how much you "dig" as a way of coping with life. This questionnaire was developed by Hayes and his colleagues (1999). For each pair of beliefs, please check the one that best fits how you feel.

The term "painful moments" is a very general word that we use to describe painful situations (e.g., parents divorcing, failing an exam, car accidents, etc.), feelings (e.g., sad, angry, scared), and thoughts (e.g., self-critical thoughts, thinking life is hopeless, upsetting memories).

_____ 1a. Painful moments will hurt you if you don't do something to get rid of them.

_____ 1b. Painful moments can't hurt you, even if they feel bad.

_____ 2a. When painful moments occur, the goal is to do something to get them under control so they hurt less.

_____ 2b. It causes problems to try to control painful moments. The goal is to let them be there, and they will change as a natural part of living.

_____ 3a. The way to handle painful moments is to understand why I'm having them, and then use that knowledge to eliminate them.

_____ 3b. The way to handle painful moments is to notice they are present without necessarily analyzing or judging them.

_____ 4a. The way to be "healthy" is to learn better and better ways to control and eliminate painful moments.

_____ 4b. The way to be "healthy" is to learn to have painful moments and to live effectively with them.

_____ 5a. Being unable to control or eliminate a painful moment is a sign of weakness.

____ 5b. Needing to control a painful moment is a problem.

____ 6a. Painful moments are a clear sign of personal failure.

____ 6b. Painful moments are an inevitable part of living.

____ 7a. People who are in control of their lives can control how they react and feel.

____ 7b. People who are in control of their lives do not need to control how they react and feel.

What are your results? Count the number of times you selected option "A" and count the number of times you selected option "B."

Option A Total _____

Option B Total _____

If you selected option "A" four times or more, it is likely that you are someone who digs herself into deeper and deeper holes. It will be helpful for you to retake this questionnaire after you complete this workbook to assess your progress. An additional copy of this questionnaire is provided in chapter 14.

What We *Can* and Can *Not* Control

If you are someone who tries to control your unwanted thoughts and feelings, you are not alone. There are several reasons why many of us like control and prefer it to other coping styles. First, society sends the message that being in control of emotions is the way to go, and the more you control your thoughts and feelings, the better off you will be.

As a result, you may have been taught to use ineffective control strategies. For instance, did it ever work when anyone told you "stop crying," "don't be afraid," or "don't be sad"? Did you feel any different after you heard such words? Can your emotions really be turned on and off like that? We suspect that these suggestions did not really work well. It's obviously not that easy. Such statements also send you the message that your emotions are "bad" and must be avoided or escaped from.

That is not always true. Sadness, anger, fear, and other emotions are often normal reactions to difficult situations. For example, one of our clients, Ashley, cried frequently during sessions, and she kept apologizing for being so "weak." Her dad had recently passed away, and we thought her tears were a sign of natural, healthy sadness rather than a pathological weakness. Ashley needed to express and experience her grief. Given that her situation was quite sad, we would have been more concerned about her well-being if she had *not* been crying.

In the case of Dolly, described previously, she felt helpless when her parents divorced. Rather than accepting that helpless feelings arise in difficult family situations, she chose to diet to ease her feelings of helplessness. Like Dolly, you also may experience thoughts and feelings that you don't want.

This is what we call "the spark plug maintenance" approach: take out the old plugs and replace them with new ones. The problem is the new ones don't always work either, or they may burn out and soon you may have to replace them again. In the previous case examples, Natalie attempts to replace her old spark plug thought "I am a failure" with the new spark plug thought "I succeed when I diet." Susan attempted to change her frustration over not being able to keep up with her friends by thinking, "They can't beat me at dieting."

The Spark Plug Mind Maintenance Approach

We do all sorts of things to change the spark plugs in our minds. Think about your own situation. In the space below, write down how you try to change or replace your thoughts and feelings.

Do you want to get rid of your thoughts about your body, your looks, or just yourself as a person? What other thoughts (spark plugs) have you attempted to replace them with? How has that worked?

Old Spark Plug	**New Spark Plug**
(Thought/Feeling to Change)	(Change by Dieting)
Example: *My body is disgusting.*	*My body will be acceptable if I lose ten pounds.*
Example: *People don't like me.*	*They will like me if I'm prettier/thinner.*
Example: *I am a failure.*	*I am successful when I diet.*
_____	_____
_____	_____
_____	_____

What Is Control?

Why is it that you and so many others try to lose weight so desperately? Could it be your way to gain control over the thoughts and feelings about yourself that you don't like? Dieting may have become your coping skill, your way of trying to escape from how you feel about yourself.

You probably behave this way because taking control does work well in certain situations. For example, if you no longer like some of your clothes, you can simply take those tops, pants, or shoes and throw them away or pass them on to someone who may actually like them. Likewise, if you are in a job that you do not like, you can simply quit that job, go to a different employer, and work there. If you are fed up with the color of the walls in your bedroom, you can simply paint the walls red, green, blue, or whatever color your heart desires.

The common element of these examples is that they all involve situations where you are in control. The important question is, what makes these situations controllable? The answer is that they all involve objects or situations in the outside world. Getting rid of things you don't like in the outside world frequently *is* possible and works well. So if you are in a controllable situation—a situation where control is physically possible—and you don't like what you've got, by all means do take charge and change what you've got!

What about controlling your thoughts and feelings? The problem is that what works well in the external world just does not work well at all in our internal world of thoughts and feelings. We often deal with our thoughts and feelings in the same way we deal with clothes we don't like. If we don't like what we think and feel, we want to throw out those thoughts and feelings.

By starving yourself to change your thoughts and feelings, you may feel better at first. Then, it seems that no matter how much weight you lose, you still feel bad and feel you "must" lose more, hoping that maybe then you will feel better. Do you recognize this pattern? Unlike old pants that go away and stay away, your thoughts and feelings keep coming back.

Remember the tug-of-war exercise? Intense dieting is one of the ways you pull away from your feelings and thoughts that you are unattractive, unsuccessful, not good enough, etc. On the one side, the thought "I am a failure" is pulling and you are fighting back with "I succeed when I lose weight." To your own dismay, you are discovering that you can't seem to win this tug-of-war. No matter how hard you try, that thought "I am a failure" always seems to keep pulling back. It just won't go away and stay away.

One of our friends discovered this the hard way. He wanted to stop cussing, and he decided to wear a rubber band around his left wrist and snap it each time he thought about cussing or said a cuss word. He figured that if he punished himself for uttering certain thoughts (cuss words), those thoughts would go away. So, each time he said a cuss word, he snapped the rubber band on his wrist. The painful, stinging feeling caused him to yell, "Oh, Shit." Oops. . . He had to snap it again. Ironically, he got the opposite of what he wanted. His thought stopping technique caused him to cuss more, not less.

By the way, the rubber band technique is not the most popular thought stopping technique out there anymore because it causes physical pain. There are, however, a number of other thought stopping techniques that some therapists still recommend. The problem is that these techniques don't really work either. Even if you can successfully suppress thoughts for a while, research shows that suppressed thoughts have a tendency to come back with a vengeance, stronger than before. This is called a rebound effect. So the bottom line is: Please don't use *any* of these techniques.

You Can't Argue With a Snake

You can't "feel better" by changing your thoughts, and you can't talk your emotions away. One reason why words are not very effective for changing our feelings has to do with the way the brain has evolved over time. The oldest part of the brain controls emotions (sadness, anger, fear), and it does not respond very well to words and reasons, such as, "I'll feel better if I only eat an orange today."

This oldest part of the brain where basic emotions are located evolved long before humans developed language. This part of the brain typically doesn't pay much attention to what our language center, the new kid on the block, has to say. In fact, the oldest part of the brain is very similar to the brain structure of lower animals like snakes and crocodiles. Have you ever tried arguing with a snake or a crocodile? Probably not, and if you ever tried, you wouldn't be sitting here reading this workbook because it wouldn't have worked and you'd be dead! You can't talk a snake or crocodile into doing anything.

Likewise, you can't change your emotions by talking to yourself in an attempt to make yourself feel better.

You Can't Run Away from Thoughts and Feelings

Georg saw an excellent example of the impossibility of trying to talk emotions away when he lived in a town in the tropical part of Australia. Every year at the beginning of the rainy season, the whole town became infested with frogs. There were frogs everywhere. Sometimes when people got in the way, the frogs jumped up at them. These unexpected "frog attacks" startled and scared some people so much that many residents developed frog phobias. In some cases, the fear was so intense that people did not want to leave their homes because they were afraid they might encounter these "disgusting" creatures.

Some people tried to talk their fear away by attempting to convince themselves that these little green frogs were absolutely harmless and could not hurt them. Yet trying to reassure themselves by replacing the spark plugs in their heads did not make a difference. It just didn't work. The fear and the disgust were still there, the feelings just were not going to change.

People could run away from frogs but they couldn't run away from their thoughts and feelings about frogs. Wherever they went, their thoughts and feelings would always be with them. It was often at this point of sheer frustration and despair that people finally sought treatment.

Luckily, you are not tormented by a frog infestation. However, you are tormented by your thoughts about food, weight, and perfection. You can't run away from those thoughts or feelings either, no matter how much you diet. Wherever you go, your thoughts and feelings will always be with you.

Experiencing Is the Answer

Although the oldest part of our brain (which controls much of our emotional response) does not respond very well to words and reason, it can learn from direct experience—and therein lies the clue to successful treatment. People must experience whatever it is that makes them afraid and whatever it is that they are running away from. So the first major step in treatment is your willingness to give up running away from the thoughts and feelings you do not like. The next step is to experience the thoughts, feelings, and situations that you fear and have anyway. In chapter 6, you will practice experiencing situations that you have avoided up until now.

You will learn to experience your thoughts and feelings the same way Georg helped the residents of tropical Australia adapt to dealing with their fear of frogs. Emotions come and go. You need not run away from your thoughts and feelings or continue your tug-of-war with them. Instead of arguing with your feelings, you will learn in the next chapter how to observe your thoughts and feelings, stay with them, and simply watch them come and go. New thoughts and feelings will emerge, and you will learn how to deal with them in exactly the same way.

We will help you develop willingness to experience your feelings of sadness, fear, and worry. Once you are willing to have what you have, you will have room to maneuver and start living a richer and less restricted life. It is one of the first steps to leading a life no longer ruled by your concerns about your body, weight, and so on.

The crucial issue and lesson to be learned here is that you can control quite a few things in the external world, but you can't control your internal world. One of the most important challenges for you (and all of us) is to understand *and* accept that. And you will learn how to accept that and move through life with all the thoughts and feelings you have.

It is crucial for us to learn to tell the difference between what we can't control and what we can control. Why is that so important? The reason is that serious problems arise when you try to control things that you have no power over, such as your thoughts and feelings. When you want to control how you feel about yourself by losing weight, you are digging. . . . And you will stay stuck in your hole. Remember: *"If you always do what you always did, you will always get what you always got"* (Hayes, Strosahl, and Wilson 1999). Fighting your thoughts and feelings hasn't worked and will not work, because it just cannot work. It's hopeless.

The Serenity Creed

Now is a good time to return to the serenity creed mentioned in the introduction of this workbook: *"Accept with serenity what you cannot change, have the courage to change what you can, and develop the wisdom to know the difference between the two."*

It is important that we follow all three aspects of the serenity creed in our lives because not doing so is likely to increase or perpetuate our suffering. We suffer most when we try to change what we have no control over. You may have hoped that losing weight would be a way for you to feel better and control how you feel. At the same time, you may already sense that this strategy has not worked well for you.

Dieting prevents you from learning to accept those situations that are beyond your control in life and that will come up from time to time, like it or not. Dieting is your way of not having what you have anyway: feelings and thoughts about yourself that you do not like. Yet your thoughts and feelings are a part of you—like it or not—and they come and go all by themselves like guests at a party. The more you don't want them, the more you will have them. The harder you fight them, the harder they fight back. The tug-of-war goes on and on and on.

The idea of controlling how you feel by losing weight is tantalizing, but this control strategy comes at a heavy cost. So the big question is: How has this strategy *really* worked for you? If you feel hopeless about this strategy at this point, we share your despair. We feel hopeless about this strategy, too.

Other Types of Control Strategies

Dieting to lose weight is probably *the* main strategy you use to gain control over what and how you feel about yourself. There are several other control strategies. The following table gives examples of control-oriented strategies that usually do not work in the long run. Please go over this table now and see which strategies you use in your life.

Strategy	Definition	Example
Avoidance Behavior	Not doing things that cause you to experience uncomfortable thoughts or feelings.	Not attending a party because you may feel embarrassed talking to other people.

Distraction	Redirecting your attention off of your primary problem and onto something else.	Developing a workaholic lifestyle.
Numbing	Trying to ease or escape from your pain.	Alcohol/Drug Use. Oversleeping.
Direct Control	Doing something to directly stop or change what is bothering you.	Trying to stop your thoughts or emotions ("Don't Cry"). Bossing other people to get them to do what you want them to.

Research Findings

Psychology researchers are aware of these control-oriented strategies, and you may be interested in learning what some of the world's top psychologists have discovered about the effects of different control strategies.

Before we summarize the research findings, we want you to have a chance to step into the shoes of these researchers and conduct a test on yourself. This test examines your mental control abilities, and we hope it will help you discover just how much you can control your thoughts.

Testing Yourself

The first step in most research is to state a hypothesis, a logical guess about what will happen. How well do you think you can control your thoughts? What is your hypothesis?

My Hypothesis:

_____

Now, you are ready to test yourself. All you have to do is *not* think about your stomach. Don't think about how it bloats when you eat. Don't think about it for even one second. Don't picture the image you see as you look down when you take a shower. Don't think of it! Or the way you have to fit into your tight jeans. Don't think of it! It's very important that you don't think of any of this.

What are the results of your test? Were you able to *not* think about your stomach at all? What happened when you tried not to think of your stomach? Perhaps your stomach did come to mind no matter how hard you tried not to think of it. If that happened to you, that was the point of this test.

We wanted you to experience that the more you tell yourself not to think about something, the more it sticks in your mind. The more you don't want something in your mind, the more you've got it. You may even still have a lingering image of your stomach right now. In real life, telling yourself to stop thinking about your body or any other situation will not stop those thoughts. In fact, as we stated earlier when we talked about thought stopping techniques, trying to suppress your thoughts will only make them stronger. Remember: *"If you don't want it, you've got it."*

More Proof: Psychological Research Findings

The test you performed on yourself is similar to research conducted by psychologists Davies and Clark (1998). They asked participants to stop thinking about upsetting thoughts. They found that the upsetting thoughts did in fact decrease, but the decrease was short-lived. At the end of the experiment, there was a rebound in the number of upsetting thoughts, and participants were experiencing *more* upsetting thoughts at the end of the experiment than they had at the beginning.

In another research study, Harvey and Bryant (1998) tested people who had been in car accidents. Half of the accident victims were told to stop thinking about the accident, and the other half were not given this instruction. *Before* the different instructions were given, both groups reported the same amount of accident-related thoughts. *After* the instructions, those who had been asked to suppress their thoughts actually experienced more thoughts about the accident than the uninstructed group.

Other researchers looked at how long college students could keep one hand in ice-cold water. Participants who tried to mentally control their pain were less tolerant of the cold water than participants who accepted the pain instead (Hayes, Bissett et al. 1999).

In our own research lab, we have seen the problem of trying to control the uncontrollable firsthand (Eifert and Heffner 2004). We wanted to see how well women could control panic symptoms such as sweating, breathlessness, and racing heart. We taught them a special breathing skill and encouraged them to use the breathing skill to conquer their panic. By now, you can probably guess what happened. Nearly half of the participants instructed to conquer their fear worried that they would lose control. Interestingly, quite a few of them (20 percent) actually did lose control—they dropped out of the study altogether. Now compare these numbers to a group of participants who we advised not to fight their symptoms and accept them instead. The results in this group were quite amazing. Participants who accepted the annoying (but harmless) panic symptoms without trying to fight them never worried about losing control and none of them dropped out of the study. By giving up their efforts to gain control, they actually had more control!

Eating Disorder Research Findings

We have discussed some studies that show you how thought stopping can be counterproductive for a variety of different problems. You may be wondering if there has been any such research directly related to eating disorders. The answer is yes, we do indeed have some research findings examining the effects of suppressing eating-related thoughts.

One of our colleagues, Cara O'Connell (2003), found that the more women restricted how much they ate, the harder it was for them to stop thinking about food, eating, and body image. Johnston, Bulik, and Anstiss (1999) conducted another interesting study. They wanted to see how stopping thoughts about food affects eating behavior. These researchers asked half of the participants to not think about chocolate while participating in a computer task to earn chocolate candies. If thought stopping really worked, then people instructed not to think about chocolate would not earn many chocolate candies when involved in a task to earn chocolate. However, people instructed not to think about chocolate actually earned more candy than the other participants who were not trying to stop thinking about chocolate.

These studies once again showed that "thought control" (suppressing, changing, eliminating unwanted thoughts) may have counterproductive effects on our behavior and produce a result that is the exact opposite of what you had hoped to achieve with that strategy. Telling yourself "don't be sad" might actually make you more sad because you will fail, as you can't talk the snake-part of your brain into feeling happier. This is the meaning of the ACT saying, *"If you don't want it, you've got it."*

What Will I Do Without Control?

As you may have come to realize, dieting is not the solution. Remember the experience of the five women earlier on in this chapter? They tried this strategy and found that it just doesn't work. Yes, you certainly can lose some more weight—you definitely can control *that*. But trying to control how you feel by starving yourself and losing weight will keep you stuck. *This* truly is hopeless: If you continue to do the same thing, you will get the same results, or as we put it earlier, *"If you always do what you always did, you will always get what you always got."*

Right now, you are digging and digging. Your hands are stuck in the soil. When you are willing to have the thoughts and feelings you have anyway—when you stop digging—you will be free to use your hands in a new, more productive way. You will literally be able to do other things with your energy, with your life. Perhaps it is time to make a bold step and take a leap of faith. Are you willing to let go of dieting and try an unknown alternative? Are you ready to do something different?

The Chinese Finger Trap

A Chinese finger trap is a tube of woven straw that is about five inches long and half an inch wide. Hayes and his colleagues (1999) used the Chinese finger trap exercise to show people how doing something unexpected and seemingly counterintuitive may be a better solution than persisting with the same old solution that does not work. Our own research on using the finger trap supports this conclusion (Eifert and Heffner 2004).

During this exercise, you are supposed to pick up the finger trap and slide in both index fingers, one finger at each end of the tube. After you fully insert your fingers, you are asked to try to pull them out. If you did that, you'd notice that the tube catches and tightens. You'd experience some discomfort as the tube squeezes your fingers and reduces circulation. You might experience some panic as you worry that you might be stuck inside the finger trap forever. You may even notice some confusion because pulling out of the tube seems the most obvious, natural way to escape. Yet it doesn't work, and you are definitely stuck if you simply just go on pulling.

How to Get Out of the Trap

The good news is that there is an alternative that does work and that will give you some space and room to move. To get there, however, you have to approach this situation differently. You have to do something that goes against the grain. Instead of pulling out, you have to push your fingers *in*. You might not get out of the trap, but pushing the fingers in will definitely give you more space to move around, more "wiggle room."

As the experience with the Chinese finger trap shows, sometimes our instinctive solutions to problems turn out to be no solutions at all. In fact, these so-called solutions may create even bigger problems. Pulling out is a very natural and seemingly logical reaction to free yourself from the finger trap, but your fingers only get caught tighter and more discomfort is created. What if we did not need to get out of the finger trap at all? What if we just created some more space for us to have what we have, to experience what there is to be experienced?

We completely understand that you would want to control painful moments and feelings in your life and change how you feel about yourself. If you keep on doing that, you will discover that dieting to gain control over your life and how you feel about yourself only creates more problems for you. It doesn't solve any problems.

The harder you pull, the more the trap tightens, and the more stuck you will be. Dieting constrains and restricts your life and doesn't create any space for you to live. In contrast, doing something counterintuitive, pushing your fingers *in* rather than *out*, will give you space and new options to make moves. So perhaps you also may have to do something seemingly counterintuitive to get yourself unstuck from where you are with your life right now.

Prepare to Let Go of the Struggle

In the next chapter of this workbook, you will actually learn to push in and do something counterintuitive: observe, accept, and lean into what you think and feel. As you learn to accept, you will free yourself and create space and opportunity to move your life in a more valued direction.

A psychologist in Spain (Luciano-Soriano et al. 2001) provides a clear, visual metaphor of a broken dam that details the ACT treatment journey you have started to embark on.

The Broken Dam Metaphor

We would like you to imagine that you are walking along a nature path. Suddenly, you notice a dam, with a crack in its wall. You don't want the dam to collapse, so you plug the hole with your finger. Although this strategy seems to work initially, it only works for a short time. Then all of a sudden another hole bursts open, and you plug it with another finger. And then another hole bursts and you use another finger. Soon, you have all of your fingers and toes covering the holes. Then the next hole bursts open, and you have to cover it with your nose. At this point you're stuck almost glued to the wall.

What kind of view do you have stuck to this wall? Can you see what is important in your life when your eyes are glued to the concrete wall? You have given your life and your body to prevent the dam from collapsing. You can't win. If you stay there glued to the wall, you will not be able to fully live your life because you aren't moving. Nothing changes; you are always in the same spot and in the same position. If you leave, you might suffer as you watch the dam collapse without being able to stop it. Some of the water and mud is going to hit you. You have to make a choice. Are you ready to move your body away from the wall *and* have the painful thoughts and emotions that may result?

In the next chapter, you will learn to watch the water spill out, without jumping in to stop it. In other words, you move on and have whatever there is to have in terms of thoughts and feelings. Once you let go of the dam, you are free to move your body in directions that you truly value.

CHAPTER 5

Learning to Be a Mindful Observer

In this chapter you will learn to:

❋ Be an observer rather than a reactor

❋ Do different mindfulness meditation techniques

❋ Listen to your thoughts and feelings without reacting to them

The intensity of competitive volleyball is not exactly the fun leisure activity you play in grandma's backyard. Throughout a volleyball match, both teams strive to keep the ball in action, back and forth from one side of the court to the other and never letting the ball hit the ground. Each time the ball is about to sail across the net to one side of the court, a player in the front row jumps up to block it with her bare hands. Behind the blocker are five other players strategically positioned to keep the ball in motion. If the ball is not blocked, a player in the back row dives to the ground with her arms stretched out to pop the ball into the air, as another teammate is set up to deliver a mighty spike to send the ball back to the other side. All the while, each player stands alert and ready, trying to read the opponents in anticipation of their next move.

Mental Volleyball

At this point, you may be wondering if this chapter is about anorexia or sports. Don't worry—volleyball does relate to anorexia. How? Well, the strategy of volleyball is a great way to describe how you are responding to thoughts about yourself. Imagine that a volleyball match is going on inside your mind. Instead of volleying a ball back and forth, the teams inside your head are volleying thoughts about you.

A Volleyball Competition with Your Thoughts and Feelings

On one side of the court is Team A "Anorexia" which serves the following thought:

You don't deserve anything nice.

Team B is ready for action, diving to the ground to prevent that thought from touching down:

I'll deserve nice things once I am more attractive.

At this point, Team A keeps the ball in motion:

You're so unattractive, how can anyone even stand to look at you, let alone like you?

Across the net, the thought goes, with Team B ready for the return:

I won't be gross once I reach 90 pounds.

Before that thought crosses the net, Team A blocks it with:

But you mess everything up.

Then, Team B powers back with:

Well, at least I'm good at dieting.

You can insert your own personal thought that Team A "Anorexia" volleys:

_____

And insert your own personal Team B response:

_____

The Players' Role

The game goes on and on. As soon as Team A "Anorexia" serves up an unsettling thought, Team B responds to that thought by committing to weight loss, purging, exercising, or dieting even harder. This volleyball competition of thoughts and feelings goes on in your head, and it also echoes in the voices of the clients we treat:

- Samantha, age nineteen, a granddaughter: *There is a battle raging inside of me. Whenever I tell myself that I'm not fat, a loud strong voice replies back telling me that if I eat I will be fat beyond repair. It is hard to hear anything except the thundering voice of anorexia shouting in my head.*

- Liz, age twenty-four, a best friend: *If I gain weight I will be so disgusting. Whenever that pig image pops into my mind, it forces me to vomit. The purging never ends.*

- Layla, age seventeen, a sister: *The disappointment I feel when I gain weight overshadows everything, even when I try to remind myself of my accomplishments.*

Like Samantha, Liz, and Layla, you may be trying hard to beat the Team A "Anorexia" thoughts by responding to every negative thought that sails toward your side of the court. However, as we discussed in chapter 4, you can not win the match. In fact, your response to everything Team A "Anorexia" delivers fires up the Anorexia Team even more. The Anorexia Team serves you an unwanted thought, and you diet in response. Determined not to let the ball hit the ground, the Anorexia Team steps up the game a notch and sends you an even more intense thought. Then you diet harder. On and on the cycle goes, with each side becoming more and more aggressive over time. Just as a volleyball player runs, dives, jumps, and pounds her body all over the court, you are exhausting yourself in this battle.

Taking a New Perspective

We're sure you agree that you deserve a break. At the same time, you probably also feel you can't just walk away and let the Anorexia Team win. At this point, we would like you to step back and think about what is going on here. You see, when you think about winning or losing, a tricky issue arises that ensures that you can actually never win this competition.

The tricky problem is that the two opposing teams are really one team: you. The thoughts on both sides of the court are YOUR thoughts. They both belong to you. No matter which side wins, one part of you will always be a loser. *You* can never win a competition where your own thoughts compete against each other. It's like waging a war against yourself. This is a war you just cannot win.

What else can you do? Is there any other way to handle your unwanted thoughts and feelings about yourself? For the longest time, you have been a player in this game. You felt compelled to do everything possible to beat the unwanted thoughts and feelings about yourself. As you work through this chapter, we hope that your role in the competition will change.

We encourage you to think about assuming a new and different role in the game than you've been playing up to now. You may wonder, "If I'm not a player, who else could I be? Perhaps a fan? Perhaps a coach?" You could certainly be a fan or even a coach. However, your problem stays the same because fans and coaches have a stake in the game. They want one side to beat the other, and, as we discussed above, it really doesn't make any sense to root for or against a part of yourself. Again, you can never be a winner in a fight against yourself.

If you wanted to let go of this unwinnable fight and not be a player anymore, then who else could you be? Have you thought about simply being the court? The court has a very important role. The game does not exist without the court because all of the action goes on there. So the court enables the game to take place.

The good news is that if you are the court, you are an impartial observer, rather than a player with a stake in the game. The court doesn't need to respond to anything. The court is merely there and watches and holds all of the players, the net, and the ball. In fact, the court does not care who wins or loses. The court does not worry about the outcome, and the court will continue to be there even after the game is over, as the players come and go.

Embrace Your Thoughts and Feelings

Occasionally, the players will pounce and dive on the court, and it is possible that the court will suffer some scuff marks and poundings. The fact that the court sometimes suffers is a valuable reminder that being an observer may sound easy but is often not easy at all. As you observe your thoughts, you will notice that some of those thoughts are painful and unpleasant. You may wish you didn't have them. You may not like what you see or feel. However, your thoughts and feelings—all of them—are a part of you. They are not *you*, but they are all a part of you.

There is another reason why it is beneficial for you to be an observer and allow all of your thoughts and feelings to be there. When it comes to suffering, you have to feel it to heal it. So unless you embrace all your thoughts and feelings, they will continue to press hard to be seen and heard.

As you learned in chapter 4, one of the most well established findings of psychological science, confirmed by many research studies, is that we cannot suppress unwanted thoughts and feelings forever, and it is simply not helpful to attempt to do so. If we do manage to suppress them, we often pay a high price for this "accomplishment." These studies have also shown that we heal from our wounds best if we allow ourselves to experience the feelings we have anyway rather than attempt to push them away.

At the same time, please remember that observers simply observe. They do not get involved in the game directly and try to influence its outcome. Also, sometimes the court needs a little extra time to heal and recuperate after a long hard battle took place. Be gentle with yourself and give yourself some extra time to heal. You deserve it.

Being an observer can be a tremendous help when you're dealing with pain and suffering. Have you ever wondered why it is easier to give advice to a friend than to yourself? It is easier to help a friend because you are an *observer* of your friend's problem. Being an observer allows you to step back rather than get all tangled up in strong thoughts and feelings.

When you think about your own situation, you may feel that your perspective is clouded by strong emotions. Being able to step back and observe gives you a clearer perspective and allows you to adopt a different approach—just as if you were doing it for a good friend. Ultimately, you have no better friend than yourself anyway.

Letting Go of the Struggle

Many clients we treat have not learned to be observers of their own struggle, and they enter therapy after they've invested considerable effort in futile struggles to numb, escape from, or deny their feelings altogether:

- Carly, age fifteen, cat owner: *My boyfriend cheated on me, and that thought keeps running through my mind. I feel miserable and keep thinking that he did that because I am too fat and that it wouldn't have happened if I were more attractive. It makes me so sick to think about this, and I want to numb these feelings and make them go away.*

- Cameron, age twenty-one, homeless shelter volunteer: *Once, I tried killing myself by cutting my wrists to escape life. Now, I'm yelling at God and pleading for this pain to go away.*

- Pam, age twenty-nine, prize-winning artist: *Wouldn't life be great if instead of numbing the pain we had a way of getting through life's pain without starving and killing ourselves?*

Like Carly and Cameron, your pain may seem overwhelming. Think about what you have done to numb your pain. Has vomiting worked? Have drugs or alcohol worked? Has losing three more pounds worked? Perhaps you felt better in the short term. Did it last or has your pain returned just as swiftly as a volleyball sails back to your side of the court?

Like Pam, you can discover that there is a way to cope with your negative thoughts and feelings without having to vomit, starve, rationalize, and chip away at your life. You don't have to numb your pain. You don't have to act on any of your thoughts and feelings, and you certainly don't have to let your thoughts and feelings dictate your actions.

What Is Mindful Observation?

Later in this chapter, you will learn to be more mindful of your thoughts and feelings. Being mindful means that you do not attempt to change your thoughts and feelings. You do not try to distract yourself, and you do not try to numb your experiences. As a mindful observer, you simply take note of whatever it is that your mind serves up for you. You watch your thoughts and feelings come and go without attempting to change them, hang on to them, or make them go away.

For instance, you could argue with your experience or you could distract yourself so that the thoughts will no longer be so intense. You could also use other means, such as drugs, to numb your unwanted experiences. The key to mindfulness is your willingness to observe and experience your thoughts and feelings without trying to hold on to them, change them, or run away from them.

Being a mindful observer has the great advantage of freeing up tremendous amounts of time and energy. Just imagine how much more time and energy you could conserve or gain if you stopped being an involved player and became a mindful observer instead. As you develop willingness, you will give yourself space and room to maneuver in different directions. Through mindfulness, you open the door to taking action so that you can move toward the most important values in your life.

Assessment: Are You an Observer?

Before we introduce you to some specific mindfulness techniques, it may be helpful for you to complete a questionnaire to see where you stand right now. Two researchers from the University of London in England, Frank Bond and David Bunce (2003), published the Acceptance and Action Questionnaire (AAQ).

By completing the questionnaire, you will learn the answers to several important questions.

- Are you someone who is willing to experience your thoughts and feelings?

- Are you someone who allows thoughts and feelings to dictate how you live your life?

- Are you ready to take action to improve the quality of your life?

We recommend that you complete the AAQ now and periodically after you have learned and practiced the mindfulness techniques for some time. Re-assessment will allow you to assess your progress. An additional copy of the questionnaire is provided in chapter 14. After reading each of the following statements, circle the number in the column that best reflects how true that statement is for you.

Part I. Willingness

Statement	Never True	Very Rarely True	Seldom True	Some-times True	Fre-quently True	Almost Always True	Always True
I try to suppress thoughts and feelings that I don't like by just not thinking about them.	7	6	5	4	3	2	1
It's okay to feel depressed or anxious.	1	2	3	4	5	6	7
I try hard to avoid feeling depressed or anxious.	7	6	5	4	3	2	1
If I could magically remove all the painful experiences I've had in my life, I would do so.	7	6	5	4	3	2	1
I rarely worry about getting my anxieties, worries, and feelings under control.	1	2	3	4	5	6	7
Anxiety is bad.	7	6	5	4	3	2	1
I'm not afraid of my feelings.	1	2	3	4	5	6	7

Part II. Action

Statement	Never True	Very Rarely True	Seldom True	Some-times True	Fre-quently True	Almost Always True	Always True
I'm in control of my life.	1	2	3	4	5	6	7
In order for me to do something important, I have to have all my doubts worked out.	7	6	5	4	3	2	1
If I get bored with a task, I can still complete it.	1	2	3	4	5	6	7

Worries can get in the way of my success.	7	6	5	4	3	2	1
I should act according to my feelings at the time.	7	6	5	4	3	2	1
I am able to take action on a problem even if I am uncertain what is the right thing to do.	1	2	3	4	5	6	7
If I promised to do something, I'll do it, even if I later don't feel like it.	1	2	3	4	5	6	7
When I feel depressed or anxious, I am unable to take care of my responsibilities.	7	6	5	4	3	2	1
Despite doubts, I feel as though I can set a course in my life and then stick to it.	1	2	3	4	5	6	7

AAQ Scoring

After you have completed the AAQ by circling a number for each item, please add the numbers you circled in Part I.

Part I (Willingness) Total _____

Higher scores reflect greater willingness to experience, rather than numb or suppress, painful thoughts and feelings. Many clients with anorexia have low scores because they try to numb, avoid, and suppress what they think and feel—particularly what they think and feel about their body and the way they look. As you progress through the mindfulness procedures and practice being an observer of your thoughts and feelings, your scores on this questionnaire may increase because you will build a greater willingness to experience distress.

Now add the numbers you circled in Part II.

Part II (Action) Total _____

Higher scores reflect greater ability to take action, even when you experience thoughts and feelings that you would rather not have. In other words, higher scores mean that you can act and do things with your life even if you don't feel good, as opposed to acting only when you feel good about yourself and your body. Many clients with anorexia have low scores because they focus so much energy on trying to be thin that they lose sight of other important parts of their life. They also feel that they can only act effectively if they first look good enough and feel better about themselves. As you progress through the mindfulness and valued directions chapters, your scores on this part of the questionnaire may also increase.

Part III Total Score _____

Unfortunately we do not yet have average scores for the AAQ from a large number of people with anorexia. However, if you add your Willingness total score to your Action total score, you can compare that number to the average score found in the study by Bond and Bunce (2003). These researchers found an average AAQ total score of 58 in a group of regular customer service center employees in England.

An Introduction to Mindful Observation

Mindful observation is a new way for you to experience your thoughts and feelings. In the past, you have been a reactor. When you experienced an uncomfortable thought or feeling, you reacted in ways to stop the thought or numb the feeling.

In this exercise, you will be an observer. You can think of yourself as the court of the volleyball match: You look up at the action and do not interfere with the game or take sides in any way. Instead, you just hold all of your thoughts and feelings.

Before you practice the mindfulness techniques, there are some important comments we want to make.

You Are Familiar with Mindfulness

First, you may have never heard the word "mindfulness" or "mindful observation" before reading this chapter. However, these techniques are not new to you. In fact, you have participated in mindfulness exercises without realizing it.

For example, when you go outside to get some fresh air, you fully observe the environment around you. Feel the cool air against your skin, smell the scent of fresh flowers, notice the sound of birds singing, feel the hot sun beating down on your face, hear the rumbling of traffic. Being present, being aware, and allowing yourself to experience everything: That is mindfulness.

The Monkey Mind

Second, it is very common for your mind to wander during mindful observation. Some people call this "monkey mind" because the thoughts in your head bounce around like a bunch of chattering monkeys swinging from tree to tree. Like a monkey at the zoo, the thoughts inside your head chatter and jump from thought to thought. Many people notice that their mind wanders off in all sorts of directions when they try to be mindful. If you notice that your mind wanders, accept that this is a normal phenomenon and then bring your attention back to the task at hand.

Judgments May Arise

Third, remember that the volleyball court does not judge the players. Mindfulness exercises are designed so that you experience *all* thoughts and feelings without categorizing your thoughts and feelings as "good" or "bad." Sometimes, as people practice mindfulness exercises, they start to evaluate their observations.

For example, you might have the thought, "I hate my body." Then, as you notice that thought, you begin to react and evaluate: "I shouldn't be thinking bad thoughts about myself." In another case, you might have the thought, "I'm not doing this right."

Then, as you notice that thought, you begin to evaluate it: "If I'm thinking this is wrong, then I must be doing something bad."

If you catch yourself evaluating your experiences as good or bad, step back into the observer role and begin to notice those judgments as just another example of your thoughts. The fact that judgments arise does not mean they are facts that you need to buy into. Evaluations are just *thinking*.

Pain May Arise

In some cases, you may observe painful thoughts, feelings, and memories. One of the goals of the mindfulness exercises is to help you learn to experience such distress. As we said earlier in this chapter, "You need to feel it before you heal it."

One way we like to describe this phenomenon to clients is by using a freezing fingers metaphor. If you live in a cold climate, you have probably experienced a time when you spent too much time outside and your hands became cold and numb. As you left the cold winter environment and returned to your warm home, the numbness began to wear off, and it hurt.

Mindful observation works in a similar way. Your emotions are frozen and numb. As you allow them to thaw out, you may experience some discomfort. And what is true for the frozen fingers is also true for your emotions: It is better to thaw them and let them heal—all the while hurting—than to keep them frozen and eventually suffer permanent frostbite damage.

Feel *Better* Versus *Feel* Better

Finally, we want to make it clear that mindful observation is not intended to help you feel *better* about yourself or get rid of any upsetting thoughts and feelings. This is an important message from us to you. Many people mistakenly believe that mindful observation is a technique to help them feel more relaxed or happier.

In ACT we emphasize that the purpose of mindful observation is to *feel* better, not to feel *better*. Those sets of words may look the same to you. However, *feeling* better means to notice and observe the feelings you experience, and some of those feelings may feel "better" or more comfortable to you than other feelings you experience.

On the other hand, feeling *better* means expecting or wanting to experience certain feelings, such as happiness, courage, or any other types of pleasant emotions. These feelings may show up for you or they may not.

We encourage you to experience what you think and feel—*all* of what you think and feel. Don't expect to achieve any particular feelings.

Why Learn Mindful Observation?

John T. Blackledge, an ACT therapist, has provided us with a good summary of reasons why people may find mindfulness helpful (personal communication, 2003). Here is what mindful observation will teach you:

Live in the moment. We often neglect to cherish the present when we experience regrets about the past and worries for the future. Mindfulness is a great way to learn how to stay grounded in the here and now and focus on what you can do now. You will learn to savor the moment.

Experience unpleasant feelings and thoughts. Before reading this workbook, you probably wanted to get rid of unpleasant thoughts and feelings because you believed they indicate there is something wrong with you that must be fixed. The end result of trying to fix or numb your thoughts and feelings has been continued distress for you. Mindfulness provides an alternative to all of these fixing and numbing techniques. This is your chance to see what happens when you do *not* struggle to get rid of your thoughts and feelings.

People who wholeheartedly engage in mindful observation say that simply observing thoughts and feelings is not as uncomfortable as you might expect. Plus, mindful observation comes at a lower cost than dieting or other control strategies you use to get rid of your thoughts and feelings.

Mindfulness gives you enhanced insight into what kinds of feelings you try to avoid, how you try to avoid them, and how much these avoidance attempts cost. As we mentioned earlier, it also teaches you that you don't have to avoid and numb your thoughts and feelings in the first place!

None of your thoughts and feelings are permanent. Sometimes, we assume that the pain will never end, and we worry that we are going to feel this way forever. When you practice mindful observation, you learn that all thoughts and feelings (whether pleasant or unpleasant) ebb and flow like waves on the ocean.

Thoughts and emotions are not permanent. They pass into and out of your body and mind. They need not leave a trace (Davis, Eshelmann, and McKay 2000). Ironically, when we struggle against unpleasant feelings or otherwise try to avoid them, they usually stick around longer and become even stronger!

Experience greater peacefulness. There is no guarantee you will experience any feeling of calm or peace. Sometimes you will and sometimes you won't. Interestingly, the people who report experiencing the least amount of calm and peace are people who try overly hard to make themselves calm and relaxed through mindful observation.

We recommend that you participate in mindful observation without any expectation of serenity. If you are meant to experience a sense of calm and peace, it will happen naturally. The more you try to force it, the less likely it will actually happen.

Be less judgmental of yourself and others. You will learn that the judgments you make have little, if any, basis in fact. Your efforts to be "better than," "good enough," "more loveable," "more happy ," etc. are often at the core of your suffering (especially when you think you have fallen short). Learning to buy into them less and less is a very productive process.

Learn that your mind isn't very good at describing your experience. Imagine talking to someone about a trip you took to a place where that person has never been. What exactly was it like to actually be there? How close does your description come to the actual experience? It seems pretty safe to say, "Not very close at all."

You've probably been through similar situations in which you tried to describe an experience to a friend who just did not connect to what you were saying. You finally concluded, "Well, I guess you just had to be there." Direct experience is simply a lot bigger, and a lot different, than words can convey.

More to the point, seemingly unpleasant situations, such as gaining weight, are often very different from what our minds tell us they will be. Usually, these situations or events are more bearable, less destructive, and more vitalizing than the struggle to numb your thoughts and feelings. The only way to know if certain situations will be as horrific as your mind suggests is to actually experience the situation and decide based on your experience. We will work on that in the next chapter.

Thoughts are just words and words are just sounds. Say the word "fat." When you first say the word, it brings up a lot of feelings and images. It's as if the word "fat" is right there in the room with you. You can just feel what it would be like to touch the blubbery texture of fat or see the white milky shine of fat.

Now say the word "fat" over and over again, out loud, as quickly as you can for about a minute. You must actually say it out loud for this exercise to work: Fat . . . Fat . . . Fat . . . Fat . . . Fat . . . Fat . . . After you've repeated the word for a minute or so, you only hear the actual sound.

Where did all the fat go? It seems to be gone. You now experience "fat" as just a sound rather than a visual image accompanied by an intense feeling of disgust. Your strong reaction to the word fat (and other thoughts that torment you) fades when you learn to allow "fat" to be there as it is (a sound) not as your mind says it is (something disgusting that you must avoid). Try it—remember you have to do it and experience it to make a difference for you.

Learn equanimity. The essence of mindful observation is to focus your awareness on what is happening right now and open your mind to "what is" (Davis, Eshelmann, and McKay 2000). When you do this, you will notice that the extreme highs and extreme lows of your emotional response to food and your body and yourself as a person, will gradually disappear. You will live life with greater balance. That is indeed a great reward of continued practice.

Preparing to Be Mindful

Before we start teaching you specific mindful observation exercises, you have to prepare.

Making a Commitment

Your first step is a commitment to practice mindful observation. As is the case with most other skills we learn in life, the benefits of mindful observation increase over time with practice. We recommend that you practice for fifteen minutes daily. For some people, fifteen minutes daily is too much and for others it is not enough. You may find that as you become more adept at mindful observation, you want to increase the time you practice. Of course, that is perfectly fine. You may even want to practice more than once a day. That is fine, too. At this early stage, however, we want you to set a realistic goal that meets your current needs. A realistic goal is a goal that you can reach with reasonable effort.

- How many times per week, and on what days, do you plan to practice?

   Number of Times Per Week: _____

   Which Days: _____

- How many minutes per occasion do you plan to practice?

    Minutes: _____

Congratulations! You have made a commitment toward your recovery! It is very important that you keep the commitment you just made to yourself. At some point, you may begin to think, "I don't feel like practicing today," or, "I don't get anything out of it anymore."

Sticking to your mindfulness practice goal is a great example of learning to behave as you choose. Practice as you plan, not as your thoughts and feelings dictate. The days you practice mindful observation even when you think, "I don't feel like practicing today," are special opportunity days in which you will reap the benefits of being mindful, and also experience the liberation of not being controlled by your thoughts and feelings. Even if you feel discouraged, be gentle with yourself and go back to your practice.

Selecting a Location

Your first step is to select a comfortable, quiet location to practice. Some people like to practice mindful observation in their bedroom. Some like to sit in a rocking chair next to a fireplace. Other people like to be outdoors, on a porch swing or near a stream.

Your job is to select a location where you feel comfortable and distraction is limited. If you choose to practice inside a room in your home, you may want to post a "Do Not Disturb" sign on the door.

A comfortable, quiet location where I can practice mindful observation is:

_____

Body Position

Much has been said and written about the right posture or position to use when practicing mindful observation techniques like meditation. Sometimes beginners become intimidated when they see others meditating in complicated special positions such as the full lotus yoga position.

Such things really do not matter for the purpose of learning to become a mindful observer. The only thing we firmly recommend is that you *not* lie down when you practice mindful observation, because you may accidentally fall asleep if you lie down.

Below are two simple postures that should work for just about anyone. We suggest you try them both out and then stick with the one that is most comfortable for you:

- Sit in a chair with your knees comfortably apart, your legs uncrossed, and your hands resting in your lap.

- Sit cross-legged on the floor. This position is most comfortable and stable when a cushion is placed under your buttocks so that both knees touch the floor.

Centering Yourself

Before you begin mindful observation, we recommend you spend a bit of time centering and grounding yourself. Be mindful of your surroundings. To do so, get settled into your chair or your cushion and close your eyes. First, turn your attention to yourself inside the room. Picture the room and some of the things inside the room. Picture the walls, the floor, the door. Next, notice any sounds that may occur inside the room . . . and outside. Notice any smells in the room. Now picture yourself in this room. Notice how you are sitting in your chair or cushion. Then focus on the place where your body touches the chair or cushion. What are the sensations there? How does it feel to sit where you sit? See whether you can notice exactly the shape that is made by the parts of your body that touch the chair or cushion. Next, notice the places where your body touches itself. Where are your hands? Notice the spot where your hands touch your legs. What about your feet—are they crossed? How do they feel in the position that they are in? What sensations can you notice in the rest of your body?

Mindful Observation Exercises

We will now take you step-by-step through three mindfulness exercises. The first one will focus on your breathing, the second one will focus on your thoughts, and the third one will focus on your emotions.

Mindfulness of Breath

One of the most basic and simple ways to be a mindful observer is to sit down and focus on your breath. Below are some specific instructions on how to do this.

1. Go to the location you selected, choose a comfortable sitting posture, and then center yourself, as described above.

2. Close your eyes and focus on your breathing.

3. Bringing your attention to the gentle rising and falling of your breath in your chest and belly. Like ocean waves coming in and out, your breath is always there. Notice each breath. Focus on each inhale and exhale. Observe the cool air pass through your nose. Feel your diaphragm (stomach) expand. Imagine your lungs fill like a balloon. Listen to the sound of your exhale. Stay focused on your breathing . . . how you inhale and exhale.

4. If you notice your monkey mind wandering off and thinking all sorts of thoughts, accept it as a natural phenomenon. Then, gently bring your attention back to rest upon your breath. Again, focus on the rising and falling of your breath in your chest and belly. Ride the waves of your breath and let your breath begin to anchor you to the present moment.

5. If you find yourself becoming distracted by bodily sensations and feelings, notice them and acknowledge their presence. Do not try to hold on to them or make them go away. Allow them to be, watch them dissipate, and gently bring your attention back to rest upon your breath.

6. A good way to deal with feelings is to name them as you notice them. For instance, if you notice you are worrying, silently say to yourself, "worry, worry, worry, there is worry." You can do the same with other thoughts and feelings and just name them as *planning, reminiscing, longing,* or whatever else you experience. Label the thought or emotion and move on. This will help you experience the difference between yourself and your thoughts. You have thoughts and

feelings but you are not what those thoughts and feelings say, no matter how persistent or intense they may be.

Mindfulness of Thought

The following exercises are found in many cultures in one form or another, and we are grateful to psychologists Davis, Eshelman, and McKay (2000) for allowing us to adopt their script from their *Relaxation and Stress Reduction Workbook* for the purposes of this book. Incidentally, if you want to learn more about mindful observation techniques, we recommend reading chapter 5 of that workbook. It provides a host of information on mindfulness and its benefits.

Your task in this exercise is to observe passively the flow of your thoughts, one after another, without trying to figure out their meaning or their relationship to one another. This will allow you to see what is on your mind and then let it go.

1. Go to the meditation location you selected, choose a comfortable sitting posture, and center yourself.

2. Close your eyes. Imagine yourself sitting at the bottom of a deep pool of water. When you have a thought, see it written on a bubble and let it rise away from you and disappear. When it's gone, wait for the next one to appear and repeat the process. Just observe the thought bubbles. Sometimes the same bubble may come up many times, or several bubbles will seem related to each other, or the bubbles will be empty. That's all okay. Just watch the bubbles come and go in front of your mind's eye.

3. As an alternative, you can imagine sitting next to a stream and watching each leaf drift slowly downstream. Observe one thought at a time on each leaf and then let each leaf drift out of sight. Return to gazing at the river, waiting for the next leaf to float by with a new thought. Think whatever thoughts you think and allow them to flow freely on each leaf. One by one. Imagine your thoughts floating by like leaves down a stream. Allow yourself to take the perspective of the stream. Hold each of the leaves and notice the thought that each leaf carries as it sails by. Just let them flow.

4. Another alternative is to imagine your thoughts rising in puffs of smoke from a campfire. Some sample thoughts you might experience include:

   - "I must lose more weight."
   - "I am breathing slowly."
   - "I am too fat."
   - "Food is poison."
   - "The room temperature is hot."
   - "I enjoy this location."

The important thing to remember while doing any of these exercises is that if you find yourself becoming distracted by thoughts and feelings, simply notice them and acknowledge their presence. Do not try to force them to go away. Gently bring your attention back to rest upon your breath, and let your breath be your anchor to this present moment.

When you complete the mindful observation exercises, gently open your eyes, pause for a while, and then do whatever needs to be done, as you continue with the rest of your day.

Mindfulness of Emotion

We have mentioned before how people with anorexia often try to block off and avoid feeling emotional pain and discomfort. You may experience sadness, anger, hopelessness, and other feelings when:

- You eat too little or too much

- You eat a "forbidden food"

- Other people treat you poorly

- You think about all of your problems

- Add your own: _____

Please remember that the more you resist experiencing your discomfort, the more it hurts. And the more it hurts, the more you may be tempted to try to resist it. This vicious circle produces one big knot of emotional discomfort and resistance that is difficult to untie.

An alternative way to deal with emotional discomfort is to learn to experience it. This means you first acknowledge the presence of discomfort, and then simply allow yourself to experience, physically and mentally, whatever it is that hurts. To help you cope with emotional discomfort, you can complete the following mindful observation exercise which has also been adapted from the *Relaxation and Stress Reduction Workbook* (Davis, Eshelman, and McKay 2000).

1. Go to the meditation location you selected, choose a comfortable sitting posture, and center yourself.

2. Close your eyes and notice the presence of discomfort, and then simply allow yourself to experience the discomfort and whatever comes along with it.

3. Sit with yourself compassionately as you experience these sensations of discomfort. Hold your own hand as you sit with yourself. Notice your discomfort and stay with it for a while. Do not try to do anything about your discomfort to make it go away. Just notice it and sit with it without judging yourself or putting yourself down for having it. Simply have what there is to have.

4. When you find yourself starting to think about other things, or if you notice any changes in how you feel, then simply notice these changes and acknowledge them. Simply watch with compassion and curiosity what happens next.

5. When time is up, gently bring your attention back to your breathing and rest your attention upon your breath. After a little while longer, open your eyes, pause for a while, and then do whatever needs to be done.

Listen to Your Thoughts and Feelings

There are two other exercises you can try out. These exercises are called "Take Your Mind for a Walk" and "Listen to Your Thoughts." Both of the exercises can help you to become an observer of your thoughts and feelings. We recommend that you sample each one of these. They both can help you to improve your mindfulness skills.

Take Your Mind for a Walk

The first exercise provides you with an opportunity to practice observing your thoughts. The point of this exercise is for you to learn how to separate your behavior from your thoughts and feelings. You can have thoughts and feelings without needing to do what they say.

In actual sessions with our clients, we do an exercise called "Take Your Mind for a Walk" that was first described by Steven Hayes and his colleagues (1999). In this exercise, we follow a client around and pretend to be the client's mind. We make judgmental statements (for example, the weather is nice; your shoes are ugly) and give directions (such as, take a right here; move faster). The client's task is to just listen to our statements. For example, just because we say "take a right here" does not mean that the client must make a right. If the client wants to continue moving straight ahead, she can choose to do that. If she wants to go right, she can choose that direction too. The point is that she is ultimately in control, not the chattering voice in the back.

We may even say out loud in a strong voice statements that are likely to make her feel uncomfortable (for instance, "I hope no one notices how gross you look today"). Again, the client's task is to listen to such statements. When she hears that thought, she can choose how to respond to it.

- She could respond with, "I hope no one notices how gross I look. I'd better not go out anymore."

- Or she can say, "Yes. I don't like it when other people think I look gross *and* I am going to continue moving in the direction I choose."

Which scenario describes your own reaction?

Unfortunately, as a workbook reader, you may not have the opportunity to have a therapist follow you around to act as your mind. However, if you have a trusted friend, you can ask your friend to volunteer to help you practice this exercise. Your friend can assume the role of the voice in your mind and follow you around with directions and judgments. It may help if you provide your friend with a list of thoughts your mind commonly feeds to you. Whenever your friend makes a judgmental comment or gives you a direction, your task is to notice it and choose whether or not to respond to it.

If you prefer to do this exercise alone, we recommend you tape record yourself stating a variety of judgments and directions. Include thoughts that make you feel uncomfortable. You can listen to the tape-recorded message as you take a walk.

We realize that this is a difficult exercise because you may feel compelled to respond to these statements in one way or another. The purpose of this exercise is to break this habit so you can simply notice them as thoughts and statements. The important thing for you is to stay on your chosen path—no matter what your mind feeds you.

Listening to Your Thoughts

What are you thinking? Using a tape recorder, record yourself speaking your thoughts. Be sure to include thoughts about your weight, body shape, self-worth, etc. After you have recorded your thoughts, play them back and listen to them. Again, at first you will probably find that this is a very uncomfortable task.

If that task is uncomfortable for you, we have some good news for you: The more uncomfortable you are with speaking and hearing your thoughts, the more therapeutic this exercise will be for you. Be sure to maintain your observer perspective, and just notice and listen to your thoughts. Don't stop the tape if you feel uncomfortable. This is your chance to see what happens when you don't struggle to get rid of your discomfort.

You Can Do It!

Once again, we would like to remind you to be patient with yourself. You do not have to be perfect. At times, you will find it difficult to do these exercises and follow the instructions. Mindful observation is a process. Changes will occur gradually over time.

Eventually, you will learn to live in the present moment and focus your attention on what you are doing right now. Continued practice will enable you to develop a less combative relationship with yourself and your nagging thoughts about your body, weight, diet, self-worth, uncomfortable feelings, external stressors, or physical discomfort.

When you fully open up to what is present, without resisting it or pushing it away, you will cultivate a deep acceptance and ability to rest more fully in the present moment. Use a gentle, nonjudgmental, and embracing attitude to encounter whatever arises during the course of mindful observation. Mindfulness is a great way to train yourself to deal with anorexia-related thoughts and feelings in your life.

CHAPTER 6

Approach Difficult
Situations with
Acceptance

In this chapter you will learn to:

✳ Tell the difference between acceptance and resignation

✳ Understand that strong feelings are not facts

✳ Practice acceptance and mindfulness in difficult situations

What Is Acceptance?

One of the most important themes of this chapter (and the entire workbook) is acceptance and learning to accept yourself with all your flaws, weaknesses, strengths, and talents—the whole package. When some people hear the word "acceptance" they think acceptance means giving in or even giving up and losing. Giving in or giving up is what we call *passive acceptance* or resignation. Please note that this is not what this chapter is about. We certainly don't want you to give up.

This chapter is about *active acceptance*. There is a big difference between these two types of acceptance. To differentiate passive versus active acceptance, let us go back to the serenity creed, "*Accept with serenity what you cannot change, have the courage to change what you can, and develop the wisdom to know the difference between the two.*"

In this book, we define passive acceptance as failing to muster the courage to change what you can. Passive acceptance or resignation is when you just give up and take no action in areas of your life that you can control. For instance, if you are a student and you decide not to go to class because you fear what others might think of you when they look at you, that would mean letting your feelings (which you cannot control) guide your actions (which you can control). This type of passive acceptance and resignation is what we do *not* want you to do, because it narrows and limits your life.

In contrast, active acceptance means letting go of your struggle with what you cannot control. As we mentioned in previous chapters, these are the thoughts and feelings you have about yourself, many of which you probably do not like very much and would rather not have. Active acceptance means mindfully acknowledging your thoughts and feelings without taking them as facts or doing anything about them. By adopting this type of acceptance approach, you free up a lot of energy and time that you might otherwise waste on attempting to change what you cannot change anyway. Active acceptance liberates you to regain the courage to take action toward what you truly can control.

The reason why we refer to this type of acceptance as "active acceptance" is that you must be willing to experience thoughts, situations, and emotions that you have strived to avoid. This is why active acceptance is a challenging task. Mindful observation helps you face this challenge because mindfulness exercises provide you with practice in this type of acceptance. As a result, you gradually learn to apply mindful observation to thoughts and feelings that you experience in everyday life.

Active Acceptance: Walk Away from a Broken Machine

Let us give you an example of active acceptance. As you read through this example, notice how the client learned to let go of an ineffective way to control and began to actively do things differently. The client, Shannon, was a nursing student at the university where we worked.

During our first session, Shannon said that she felt her mother did not care about her. Throughout childhood, Shannon had tried hard to please her mom. Shannon excelled as a competitive swimmer, but mom never came to the meets. Shannon took college-level courses as a high school student, but mom only complained about the cost of the tuition. Nothing Shannon did was ever good enough to earn mom's attention and praise.

Shannon said she needed to diet because mom would like her more if she were thin. Maybe mom would finally be proud enough to put her arm around Shannon or brag about Shannon to her friends. Although everything else Shannon did to get mom's attention failed, Shannon assumed anorexia would be her ticket to a better relationship with mom.

At our second session with Shannon, we planned to address her problem with her mother further. Before we began, Shannon told us that the soda machine in the first floor hallway had just eaten her money. Shannon had gone to the snack area to quench her thirst. She properly inserted her dollar bill and made a selection. The soda machine rattled, but nothing came out. So, she inserted more and more money. She hit the "coin return" button but no money was returned. Then, she started to curse at the machine. In a fit of frustration, she shook and hit the machine. No matter how much time, energy, and money Shannon invested, the soda would not come out. The machine was clearly broken. Shannon had to choose whether to continue to fight all day with the soda machine or accept her loss and walk away toward more fulfilling activities in her life. She could continue to invest time, energy, and more money in this machine, or she could choose to cut her losses and walk away. She chose to walk away and give up the battle against the broken machine.

In Shannon's case, we were able to connect the soda fiasco to her treatment problem. It was not her fault that the machine was broken. She did everything possible to get it to work. Yes, she deserved a soda, but fixing the machine was out of her control. Actually, a more accurate way of describing this situation is: She deserved a soda *and* fixing the machine was out of her control.

Likewise, mom was broken. Shannon deserved a loving mother *and* her mom had her own problems, which made mom unavailable to have a loving relationship with Shannon. There was nothing Shannon could do to change mom. Just as adding more money wouldn't make the soda machine work, dropping pounds wouldn't make mom more committed to the relationship with her daughter. Shannon could not control her mom's behavior.

The only thing Shannon could control was how she reacted to her mom's behavior. So, although Shannon could not change her mom, she could change her *reaction* to mom. Instead of trying to control mom's behavior by dieting, Shannon decided to accept that mom was broken, let go of efforts to make mom love her more, and focus on moving on with her life.

When Shannon returned the following week, she proudly said, "I've stopped putting money into 'the mom machine.'" Indeed, Shannon reported several examples of how she had moved away from trying and trying to win mom's praise. For example, she decided to cut her hair the way she wanted, not the way mom preferred.

Throughout treatment, Shannon continued to practice accepting her mom's behavior. She gradually let go of her desire to create the perfect body as a way to create the perfect relationship with mom. Acceptance strategies liberated Shannon because she was now focusing on many other things that mattered to her. Over time, her anorexia symptoms decreased in the sense that she was thinking less about food and her body.

Please note, however, that she would have still preferred to be slimmer, but she didn't let that desire dictate her actions and what she would do with her life. Shannon observed one other interesting and surprising consequence of her change: her relationship with her mom actually improved over time, possibly because Shannon put fewer demands on her mother, which made it easier for her mother to move a little closer to Shannon. This effect is also a nice illustration of the paradoxical effects that can happen when we stop chasing something we desperately want *and* cannot control: The more we chase it, the less we get of it; and the less we chase it, the more we may actually get of it.

Now please think about your own life. Is there a problem that you have tried and tried to control, without any results? As you go through this week, ask yourself: Are you investing your time, money, or energy in a broken machine? Is your struggle with anorexia such a broken machine? If so, how else could you invest your time, money, or energy if you walked away and let go of this problem?

Strong Feelings Are Not Facts

When clients learn acceptance by practicing mindful observation, they occasionally observe very intense emotions:

- Fear

- Sadness

- Disgust

- Confusion

As you practice mindful observation, you will learn that the strength of the emotion does not attest to the truth of that emotion. This means that no matter how strong and persistent your feelings may be, they are still feelings that come and go, and you don't have to buy into them.

For example, there will probably be times fear will show up in you. When you think about eating, you may be overcome with fear of what food will do to you. You may even experience a panic reaction as your hands shake, your heart races, and you start to sweat. Those are all emotional reactions you can mindfully observe. The reality is that no matter how strong your fear is, food is not going to hurt you.

Your fear and other emotions are definitely real in the sense that they do occur in your mind and body. Yet no matter how strong they are—or as one of our clients said, "no matter how much they yell at me"—they are not some truth or fact. Your emotion is a part of you that waxes and wanes. So let experience and values guide your way.

One of the most important lessons mindful observation teaches you is that you don't have to decide whether your feelings are right or wrong. Your task is to simply acknowledge their presence without holding onto them or pushing them away. When our clients really get into the observer role, we have heard them even thank their mind for *any* thoughts or feelings it dishes up for them, regardless of whether those thoughts and feelings are of a more pleasant or painful nature.

Practice Experiencing Difficult Situations

As you continue to practice the mindfulness exercises, the observation skills you develop will help you to be mindful when you experience situations that distress you. In the remaining sections of this chapter, you will learn to develop willingness to approach situations that you may have previously avoided. We realize that these exercises will be tough. In fact, we suspect they may turn out to be the toughest part of this workbook for you. Still, we encourage you to stay the course. We will guide you through these exercises as best we can.

You may be curious about the situations that we would like you to experience. Some situations revolve around food, some situations revolve around body image, and some situations are distressing for most people and not directly related to anorexia.

Here are some examples of situations that revolve around food:

- Eating forbidden foods

- Eating in public

- Not being able to vomit or get rid of calories

Below are some examples of situations that revolve around body image:

- Wearing revealing clothes

- Looking in the mirror

- Hearing someone comment on your appearance

Below are some examples of situations that are distressing for most people, although not directly related to anorexia:

- Performing poorly on a task

- Arguing with a friend

- Worrying about financial problems

Your Difficult Situations

Which situations distress you the most? As you make your list, try to identify situations that you will have the opportunity to experience on a regular basis. For example, death in the family is very distressing, but that is not a good choice because that (hopefully) is a rare event that does not happen on a regular basis. So, we want you to identify situations that occur relatively frequently so that you will have recurrent opportunities to practice.

Difficult situations that revolve around food:

1. _____

2. _____

3. _____

4. _____

5. _____

Difficult situations that revolve around body image:

1. _____

2. _____

3. _____

4. _____

5. _____

Difficult situations not directly related to anorexia:

1. _____

2. _____

3. _____

4. _____

5. _____

If you have any problems completing your list, you might find it helpful to look at the list below. It was compiled by Betty, age twenty-two:

Betty's Difficult Situations

Difficult situations that revolve around food:

- Eating pizza

- Eating any food if I don't know how many calories are in it

- Eating in front of other people

- Feeling "heavy" after I eat

- People arguing with me about how much I eat

Difficult situations that revolve around body image:

- Having to squeeze into my jeans

- Seeing a number on the scale that is higher than my goal weight

- Wearing a bathing suit

- Looking at my stomach

- Going to school and seeing people prettier than me

Difficult situations not directly related to anorexia:

- Being stuck in traffic

- Watching sad stories/tragedies on the news

- Feeling lonely when my friend does not call me

- Getting mad when my boss blames me when I make a mistake

- Having a bill collector call me

Approach Your Distress

After examining Betty's list and preparing your own list, you are ready to go through and experience your distressing situations in real life. Practice experiencing one situation at a time. Yes, you must actually *do* it. Hopefully, you listed situations that occur frequently enough that you will have an opportunity to practice as needed. If not, revise your list.

We suggest you start with the situation you are most comfortable approaching, and then work your way up to the most distressing situations. In this way, you are ascending a staircase of distress, going from most to least comfortable situations. Most people find that this gradual approach works best for them.

Go ahead and pick a situation now. Next, start to do what you need to do in this situation. As you go through the situation, notice your thoughts and feelings in the situation. Be an observer of your thoughts and feelings. Listen to what your mind yells at you. Just listen. Practice the mindfulness of breath, thought, and emotion exercises you learned in chapter 5. Don't use mindfulness exercises to distract yourself or to feel better. Use the exercises to be an observer of how you are reacting to being in your situation.

Some people find it helpful to pretend to be a sportscaster observing a sporting event. Using a sportscaster's voice, they give a detailed description of all the action and describe all of the thoughts, feelings, behaviors, sights, smells, sounds, tastes, and sensations. To get you started, it may help you to read a sportscaster's description that Gloria created when she practiced mindfulness while eating a slice of pizza.

Gloria's Experience While Eating Pizza

Gloria hears the knock at the door, and off she goes. She is walking slowly. Her heart is pounding, and her hands are shaking. She is thinking that she can't believe she is actually going to go through with this. Okay. Now, she's opening the door, and the delivery man is handing her the pizza box. She's feeling the warm box as it heats up her hands. Now let's watch her head off into the kitchen. She's still moving slowly, and her eyes are filling with tears. She feels really confused. The thoughts in her head are yelling to her like the chant of a crowd, and this crowd is going wild. She is listening to the crowd of thoughts yelling, "Don't eat it." "You'll be a cow." "Do you know how many calories are in one slice?" This crowd is getting louder and louder. What will Gloria do? Tears are rolling down her cheeks. This is indeed a very difficult situation for her.

Now, Gloria is taking a deep breath and exhaling. She allows herself to feel the pain, allowing those tears to flow. Now, Gloria is slowly opening the box. The smell of freshly-baked pizza is overwhelming her. She sees the pizza, and she is reaching in. She's picked a slice with a bubble in the crust. Now she's poking at the slice and feeling the slimy, cheesy texture. Her fingers feel greasy. She continues to cry. The crowd of thoughts is yelling louder than ever. This crowd wants her to get away from that pizza. Her feeling of confusion is at its strongest right now. Now, she is lifting the pizza toward her mouth. Slowly. Slowly. Slowly. Now, her mouth is opening slightly. She has just enough room to fit in the tip of the slice. Now, the pizza is in her mouth. She's starting to bite down. There it goes. Gloria has taken her first bite. She can hear the sound of her teeth grinding as she chews. She's noticing the texture of the pizza as it gets chewed around inside her mouth. There is a strong taste of tomato sauce in her mouth. Gloria is thinking about spitting it out. Wait a minute. She stopped chewing. What will she decide to do? Gloria takes another deep breath and encourages herself, "You can do this." Okay. Now, she's back to chewing. There it goes. Her first swallow. Gloria feels her throat muscles contract and relax. . . .

Riding the Wave

When Gloria started this exercise, her thoughts and feelings were very intense, and they became more and more intense as she continued and followed through. When you experience your situations, you also will probably notice that your feelings build up like a wave in the ocean. They get more and more intense. They appear bigger and bigger. Then they eventually reach their peak and just like a wave they will level off and drift away. They don't last forever.

It is critical that you ride the wave of your emotions. Once you start to go through one of the situations and you have taken that step, *you must remain in the situation* (no escaping or numbing) until the intensity of the emotion decreases. Otherwise, your fear might actually worsen. Let us remind you again how important it is to see an exercise through to the end once you have started. We suspect that during any of these situations, you will have the strong urge to stop the whole exercise and chuck it all in. If that happens, do not act on that thought and urge. This is one of the most critical moments to practice mindful observation and not act on any feelings and urges to escape that you will undoubtedly experience. Please give yourself sufficient time to experience what happens to your thoughts and feelings as you're observing them and remain in the situation until their intensity decreases.

After you experience your first situation, move on to the next and keep going until you experience all the situations on your list. Again, simply be a mindful observer or sportscaster of each situation.

Mindful Eating Exercise

You have listed five food-related situations. We encourage you to use mindful eating when you experience these situations. Use all of your senses: smell, touch, taste, sight, and sound. Listen to the thoughts you experience. Notice your emotional reaction. Observe your behavior. Be totally present.

Some people want to complete the eating exercises as quickly as possible. They shove the food in, take a quick bite, and say, "Okay. I ate one bite. I did it. It's over." That is not mindful eating. That is avoidance. The eating exercise will work best for you if you take your time and fully engage in the experience.

When some clients with anorexia begin to eat more, they are often haunted by the fear that if they start to eat again, they will never be able to stop. They fear they will eat and eat and eat until they explode. If you share that fear, you will be pleased to know that you will not overeat if you are a mindful eater.

When you mindfully observe your reactions to eating, you will learn to listen to your body. You will be more aware of when your body is hungry and *when it is full.* By staying in tune with the messages your body sends to you, you can prevent binge eating. Binge eating occurs when we ignore our body's signal to stop eating. If you would like to learn more about mindful eating, we recommend that you read *Eating Mindfully* by Susan Albers (2003).

The following worksheet can help you practice mindful eating.

Mindful Eating Worksheet

Food to Be Eaten: _____

Amount to Eat: _____

Your Location: _____

1. Use Your Senses
   - Smell: Notice how your food smells.
   - Taste: Notice how the food activates your taste buds.
   - Sight: Notice what your food looks like.
   - Sounds: Listen. Do you hear your stomach growling, chewing noises, etc.?
   - Feel: Notice the texture of your food, and notice your body's physical response to the food. Feel the food as it is chewed in your mouth. Notice how the food passes through your throat and rests in your stomach.

2. Notice Your Reactions

- Listen to the thoughts you experience. Just observe. You may find it helpful to list your thoughts:

  _____

  _____

- Notice your emotional responses. How do you feel? Describe your feelings:

  _____

  _____

- What are you doing? Describe your behavior:

  _____

  _____

- Describe your physical responses. Be aware of your whole body. Notice your breath, your heart, your stomach, your legs, your hands, your facial expression. Scan yourself from head to toe. Describe your physical responses below:

  _____

  _____

The Mirror Exercise

On your list, you included body image situations. Looking in the mirror can be very difficult for people with an eating disorder. In addition to the situations you listed, we recommend that you practice being a mindful observer when you look in the mirror. Here is what we would like you to do:

1. Use a full-length mirror.

2. View yourself naked in front of the mirror. Really look at yourself. Observe and describe your body from head to toe. Describe what you see. If you live in a location, such as a college dorm room, where it is not possible to be nude, wear the most revealing clothing you own.

3. Try to give descriptions, not judgments. If you experience judgmental thoughts, such as those listed below, notice the thoughts and feelings that arise. Just listen to them.

Judgments:
"There is too much fat on my thighs"
"I look bad."
"My body is not as attractive as my friends'."

Descriptions:
   "I want to cry when I look at my body."
   "My fingernails are painted red."
   "I can see my rib bones sticking out."

4. Allow yourself to experience those thoughts and feelings. Ride the wave of your discomfort. Stay committed to the exercise. View yourself for as long as you have planned. We recommend that you view yourself for at least five minutes. If you find after five minutes that your discomfort is still at the same level as it was when you started, we recommend that you continue with the exercise until the urge to escape from the mirror situation has passed. It is important that you stay the course. Do not give in to your discomfort and terminate the exercise prematurely.

Recording Your Thoughts and Behaviors

This exercise incorporates both mindfulness and acceptance. In the left-hand column, write down some thoughts that bother you. In the middle column, rate each one from 0 to 10, indicating how willing you are to experience the thought without reacting to it. Finally, in the right-hand column, record your behavior and reactions to each thought. We've started you off with an example so you can see how it works.

Thought	Willingness to Experience Thought (0=Not Willing, 10=Totally Willing)	Reaction/Behavior
"They're staring at me because they think I'm fat."	*1*	*Throw away the apple I bought for lunch.*

Your personal thought and behavior record can give you some valuable clues about yourself. What does your thought record indicate? When you are less willing to accept your thoughts, do you diet more? When you are willing to let your thoughts be what they are, how do you behave? Consider whether accepting your thoughts more willingly might help you move in valued directions.

The Scale Exercise

One of the most uncomfortable situations for clients with anorexia is stepping on the scale and seeing the number increase. The fear of weight gain is so intense that it prevents many clients from eating enough to recover.

In chapter 5, we talked about how thoughts are just words and words are just sounds. When it comes to weight, your weight is just a number and a number is just a sound too.

What is your goal weight (or actual weight, if you don't have a goal weight)? When you first say that number, it has a very powerful meaning to you. You can probably feel all the emotion that you associate with that number. Now, say that number out loud as fast as you can for 1 minute. You must actually say it out loud for the exercise to work. Use a kitchen timer to help you with the exercise. When the minute is up, all of the emotion is gone. All you have left is a sound.

To further help you, we recommend that you practice observing numbers on the scale. When you step on the scale, hold a heavy object in your hand, and notice the number. It may be a number that is higher than your goal weight, and that number may be very uncomfortable to view. Allow yourself to ride the wave of that discomfort. Then, add an even heavier object to your hand, and notice how the number increases even more. Again, stay on the scale and allow yourself to ride the wave of that discomfort.

An Exercise for Those Who Purge

There is a special exercise we recommend for clients who purge with diet pills, vomiting, excessive exercise, or laxative abuse. Does that describe you? If so, we want you to list your "forbidden foods." Think of three foods that trigger purging for you.

1. _____

2. _____

3. _____

Now, start with one of the three listed foods that you are most comfortable eating. Eat that food, and engage in mindful eating (see description presented earlier in this chapter). After you eat, notice the sensations, thoughts, and feelings that arise. Just listen. Ride the wave of this discomfort, allowing your urge to purge to come and go.

One client we treated, Naureen, could not resist eating pecan pie. It was her favorite treat. However, every time she ate a slice, she felt incredible guilt because she consumed so many calories. To get rid of her guilt, she forced herself to throw up. In therapy, we brought a pecan pie into the session, and each of us ate a slice. After eating the pie, Naureen practiced being an observer. She noticed how she felt bloated, and she heard the thoughts in her head that yelled, "You will explode if you don't purge." Naureen allowed her guilt, discomfort, and urge to vomit to come and go. That experience, which we repeated a few times, taught her that she did not need to react to those intense thoughts and feelings to purge. The voice that yelled, "You will explode if you don't purge" was full of hot air.

Thoughts Are Not Facts

As you experience the situations on your list, in addition to the mirror, scale, and purge situations we recommended, you will learn that you don't have to buy everything your mind says! During these exercises, your mind will be yelling very harsh words at you. Here are some examples of thoughts you may encounter during your mindful observations:

- *"There is no point in doing this because I am* never *going to get better."*

- *"I ate so much, I feel like I'm going to explode."*

- *"I am afraid that nobody will ever like me if I gain weight"*

When you encounter intense and extreme thoughts such as the ones listed above, you may buy into them and accept them as facts. With continued mindfulness practice, however, you will learn that your thoughts are not facts. Sometimes, the actual experience is not as bad as your thoughts want you to believe. As you become more mindful, you will learn that you don't have to believe your thoughts, or reject them, or argue with them. Your task is to simply observe thoughts and feelings and watch them come and go without doing anything about them.

As you observe your thoughts, you might also notice that your actual experience was not as distressing as your thoughts and feelings said it would be. One way to assess how much you buy into what your mind says is to rate, from 0 to 10, the extent to which you believe each thought or feeling is true. Zero means you believe it is absolutely not true, and 10 means you believe it is absolutely true. As you learn to be an observer of your thoughts, your experience will show you that your thoughts are not always true: People will still like you, you won't actually explode, and recovery will get easier.

The graph below demonstrates our point. When Gina first practiced the mindfulness observation exercises, her thoughts kept telling her, "If I gain weight, I will lose all self-control." After Gina practiced mindfulness techniques each day for several weeks, she began to view this thought more and more from an observer perspective. Each time she experienced this thought she rated the believability from 0 to 10. As her Believability Graph shows, the thought, "If I gain weight, I will lose all self-control," became less believable as time (and experience) progressed. Gina learned that weight gain did not lead to loss of self-control as her thoughts suggested it would.

You don't have to buy your thoughts either! A sample Believability Graph is attached for you. Select a thought that you experience and rate how much you believe the thought, from 0 to 10, each time you experience it. Does the thought become less believable over time?

Here's one final note on the believability of thoughts. After practicing mindful observation and engaging in some of the other exercises we included in this workbook, Gina and other clients found that they believed their thoughts less—but they still had the thoughts. In other words, the frequency of thoughts did not change; they only seemed less credible and they seemed to loosen much of their grip on the person over time. So please do not expect your unwanted thoughts to disappear. They may or they may not disappear. Ultimately it doesn't matter if they continue to hang around, as long as you do not act on them anymore.

How much Gina believed her thoughts

Gina's Thought: *If I gain weight, I will lose all self-control*

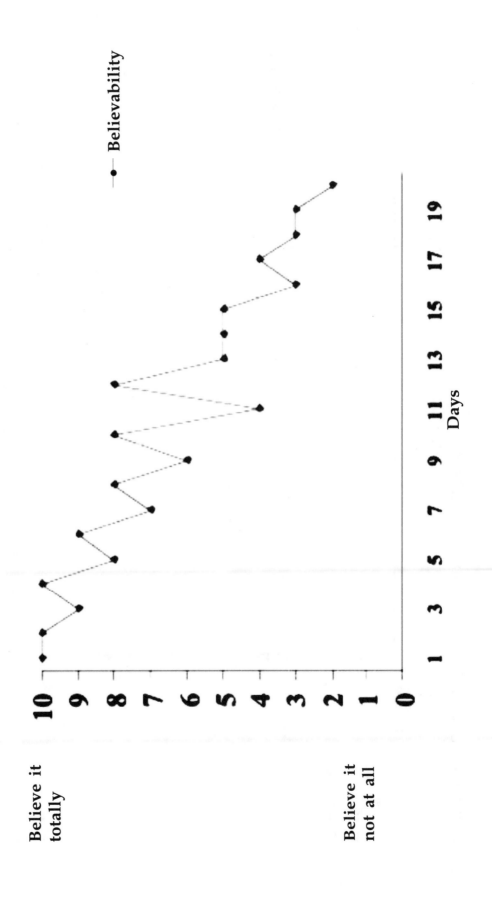

How much do you believe your thoughts?

Thought: _____

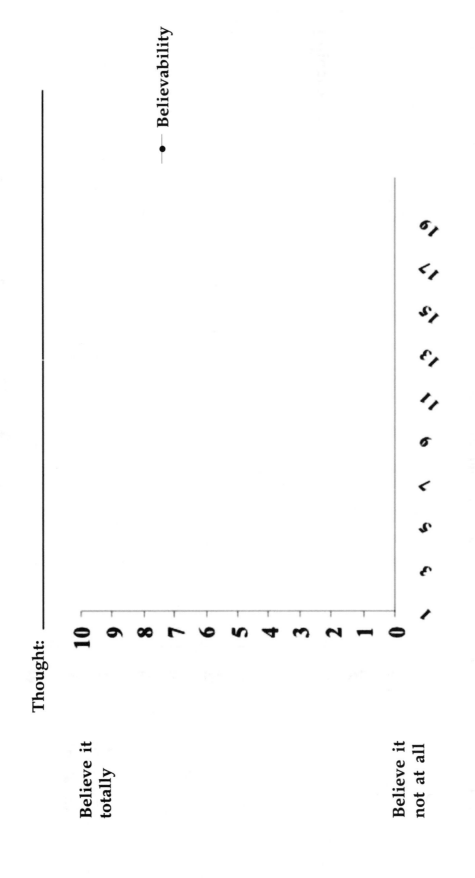

CHAPTER 7

Choosing Valued Directions

In this chapter you will learn to:

* Distinguish values from goals

* Assess if you are living a valued life

* Define what you want your life to stand for

* Commit to a valued direction

Molly, a twenty-nine-year-old musician, described anorexia as a monster growing inside of her. She wrote in her therapy journal:

When this anorexia monster first appeared, it was just a baby, but it was scary enough that I wanted it to just go away. So, I fed it to keep it at bay. The more I fed it, the bigger it got, and the more frightened I felt. I kept feeding it and feeding it, hoping it would leave me alone. Then, I realized that the monster possessed me, and it did not plan to leave. In the end, there was nothing left to feed to the monster. Nothing left except me.

The "fat" thoughts and "worthless" feelings people with anorexia experience are like a monster growing inside. Each time you diet, you feed the anorexia monster to appease and calm it. As a result, those thoughts grow bigger and bigger. The question you must ask yourself is, "Who is in control here? Who is choosing?" Is it you or is it a monster called anorexia?

We suspect that the anorexia monster has moved you away from valued life directions and put them on hold. This chapter is about reclaiming your life. You have the power to choose the direction you want your life to take. You don't have to devote your time, energy, and life to feeding the anorexia monster. Most importantly, you don't have to wait until you have "mastered your anorexia," and gotten rid of all the symptoms and problems associated with it, to move on with your life. You can learn from Molly, who ended her journal entry with:

> *The monster terrorized me for eight years. I thought my life was lost forever. Now, I have let go of that demon and the power it possessed over me. I am reminded that I am in control every time I gaze into my boyfriend's eyes, listen to the sound of the piano I play, or hold my baby niece in my arms.*

Life Without Anorexia

Have you ever wondered what your life would be like if the anorexia monster did not consume you? Use the space below to describe how your life would be different if your time were not consumed by the endless battle to be thin. If you didn't have anorexia, what would your life be like? What kind of things would you do? What would your relationships be like? Write about the life you imagine you'd be living if you didn't have anorexia.

_____

_____

_____

_____

_____

_____

_____

What Are Values?

Values are parts of life that are important to most people. You will probably notice that your values come out in the statement you just wrote. We categorize values into nine domains or areas: Family. Friends. Romantic relationships. Leisure. Education. Career. Citizenship. Health. Spirituality. Although we list domains separately, most domains overlap. For example, the value of education can lead to a career and your career can lead to meeting new friends.

Why Are Values Important?

You may wonder why we are talking about your values in a book on anorexia. In this chapter we will review some reasons why values are so important in your struggle with anorexia. We'd also like to help you start exploring your values in a systematic way to help you reclaim your life.

Values Make the Hard Work Worthwhile

In chapter 6, we asked you to do some exercises that probably were uncomfortable for you. Why did we ask you to observe thoughts and approach situations that you'd prefer to avoid? Because when you numb your thoughts or avoid situations, it limits your quality of life. We want you to live a long, fulfilling life.

As you explore valued directions in this chapter, you will rediscover, or perhaps discover for the first time, what is most important to you. Working toward values will motivate you to keep up with the hard work of therapy. The investment you make in treatment will pay off as you reclaim your life.

We Want You to Stay Driven

One of the reasons we choose to treat clients with anorexia is that we admire their strength. They are among the most driven and committed people we have ever met. Therapists enjoy working with hardworking clients who enter therapy with commitment and drive. People with anorexia are extremely driven to be thin, and they work very hard to limit how much they eat. When clients with anorexia first enter therapy, the drive is focused on being thin. Then, as we explore values, they think about how they can use their drive in a different way to be a loving sister, a good friend, a student, an athlete, or whatever else their heart desires. As you explore your values in this chapter, we'd like you to be thinking about this as well. How can you use your drive differently?

Your drive is a gift. You can think of your drive as being like a hammer. Just as you can use a hammer to build or to destroy, you can focus your drive on a commitment to being healthy or being unhealthy.

Values Give You an Alternative to Dieting

One of the most pressing concerns clients with anorexia have is, "If I give up dieting, what will I do instead?" This treatment plan is about learning that you deserve to live a full life, and it will help you find a path that will lead you in that direction. In this chapter, you will discover what you can add to your life if you choose to take out dieting.

Antonia, forty-four, Internet surfer: *Anorexia prevents me from pursuing real happiness and following my dreams. First I used to think, "I would be happy if just lost five more pounds." Then, five pounds later, I noticed I wasn't happier, and thought maybe five more pounds would do it. The biggest problem for me is that I have become so obsessed with discovering happiness from that number on the scale that I don't have time or energy left to discover pleasure from other, more rewarding things in life.*

Perhaps you can empathize with Antonia. Think of life as a walk through a corridor with many doors. You have the power to choose which doors to open and enter. One of those doors is labeled anorexia, and you have chosen the anorexia door for so long that you may have lost sight of other options that are available to you. This chapter gives you alternatives to explore. You can venture out and open up other doors. You can also choose to stay inside the anorexia room.

What choice do you want to make? When you stay locked behind the "anorexia door," it limits your life. For example, anorexia may not give you the energy you need to do things you want to do. Anorexia may worry the family members you love. Anorexia may cause you to push away friends who express concern about you.

Here is an important question: Do you want to be thin, or do you want to have your life back? Now is the time to muster the courage to explore other doors in your life corridor.

Think about your life. Besides anorexia, what other doors can you open? List them below:

1. _____

2. _____

3. _____

4. _____

5. _____

Voices of Anorexia: Examples of Valuing

When we meet with clients, we hear them express values when they talk about the most important things in their lives. Listed below are some sample statements that give you a glimpse of what clients value in each of the nine domains.

Keep in mind that these are examples. Values do differ from person to person, and your values may be quite different from the ones you read below. Also note that the values are not clearly identified yet. However, the statements point in the direction of the underlying values.

Family

- Hillary, age twenty-eight, mother of a three-year-old boy: *The most beautiful miracle for me is to hear my son say, "I love you, Mama." The sound of my child's voice expressing those four words inspires me.*

Friends

- Ruby, age sixteen, soap opera fan: *My best friend and I met in the fourth grade. She was new in town, and I was the first person to greet her when she moved to my school. I try to be friendly and welcoming, and I am so glad I approached her because we have so much fun together and make each other laugh.*

Romantic Relationships

- Julie, age thirty, registered Democrat: *My boyfriend has been so supportive. For a long time, I put up a wall and I didn't let other people in. Then, Tommy stuck by my side through everything. I took a risk to be vulnerable, and it has made a difference in my life. I have learned how to love and how to be loved.*

Leisure

- Amanda, age forty-three, survivor of domestic violence: *Somewhere deep inside, I long to pick dandelions, dance in the rain, walk through a drive-through, and sing to the stars. Each day, I take time to celebrate life.*

Citizenship

- Lucy, age twenty-one, nursing student: *I volunteer at a nursing home on Saturdays. I spend most of my day with a woman who has Alzheimer's disease. When she is crying or confused, I put my hand on her shoulder, and I whisper comforting words. She responds to my voice and my touch. It feels so good to help someone in need.*

Health

- Lyn, age fifteen, her parent's only daughter: *I spent so much time taking care of other people that I neglected to take care of myself. I now make sure my own needs are met. When I take care of myself, I am better able to take care of others.*

Spirituality

- Tammy, age thirty-nine, nutritionist: *I have turned to religion in my times of need. Prayer helps me to find an inner peace.*

Career

- Danielle, age twenty-six, veterinary assistant: *I value the gift of being able to help animals through my work. One time, we had a stray cat that we wanted to place in a loving home. He had been through a lot as a stray, so I bought him a special "purple heart" name tag for bravery to show people what a special cat he was. He found a home within two hours.*

Education

- Miranda, age twenty-four, dancer: *I always felt that people took advantage of my kindness. It hurt that I was always being stepped on. I took an assertiveness course, and I learned that it's not selfish to ask for what you deserve and need. Now I practice being assertive, and people respect me more.*

Is It a Goal or a Value?

Goals are destinations. Once you reach your goal, the work is done, and you are finished. For example, getting married is a goal. Once that ring is on your finger, your goal is achieved. Values are lifelong journeys and you never ask, "Am I done yet?" You continually pursue what you value throughout life. For example, the value of being a loving, devoted wife is not complete the moment you say "I do." Being a loving, devoted wife is something you must constantly keep on working toward.

One of the most common problems we encounter when we ask clients about their values is that they confuse goals with values. For instance, when you say, "I want to be happy", that sounds like a value, but it is not a value. Being happy is kind of an emotional goal. It is something you can either have or not have. Essentially, being happy is an outcome, a result that may (or may not) happen *after* you start moving toward your values. Values are a direction. They must be lived out (Hayes et al. 1999).

Some clients focus more on setting goals than identifying values. Wendy, for example, bought a 12-step book. She set a goal to read one chapter each week, and thought, "In just twelve weeks, all my problems will be solved." Do you think Wendy was "cured" at the end of those twelve weeks? Nope. Although she reached her reading goal, finishing the book was just one step toward her lifelong value of sound mental health.

In ACT, we do believe goal setting is important, and we always discuss goals in relation to values. In fact, this is typically a two-step process. First, after a client identifies what she values in each of the valued life domains, we encourage the client to set specific goals to progress toward those values. Again, keep in mind that reaching a particular goal is just one of many steps in a valued direction.

Another way we incorporate goals is to ask clients to identify the values that underlie their goals. For example, examine your own behavior. Think of goals you have set for yourself. To determine the value that underlies the goal, ask yourself, "Why am I doing this?" What am I trying to accomplish with this goal? Where am I heading with this?

For example, many people enroll in college. Graduating from college is a goal because you reach this destination when you have that degree in your hand. A more fundamental question to ask is: What values underlie the goal of a college education? The answer will vary among individuals depending on their values. Some people want to earn a degree because they value learning and education. Others value being financially secure, and earning a degree is a step toward a higher income. Others value friendship, and college is a way to meet new people and make friends.

Think of Your Own Life

Think of goals you have set, including long-term and short-term goals. Write them on the left lines. For each goal you've set, write on the right side line what value underlies that goal.

Goals You've Set   **Why are you doing this (value)?**

1. _____   _____

2. _____   _____

3. _____   _____

4. _____   _____

5. _____   _____

Examples

What values underlie your goals?

Goals You've Set	**Why are you doing this (value)?**
1. *I want to have children someday.*	*To nurture children and watch them grow.*
2. *I want to get an A on my next test.*	*Succeeding when challenged.*
3. *Acceptance into medical school.*	*Having a prestigious, challenging career.*
4. *Plan a party for my friend's birthday.*	*Express affection toward people I love.*
5. *Go to swimming pool once per week.*	*Enjoy meeting new people and socializing.*

The Dead Man's Goal

As you explore your personal values, the statements you write in the following exercises will guide you on the route you plan to take with your life. Imagine if you were on a trip and you asked some people for directions. Instead of telling you where to go, they told you where not to go. If they said, "Don't go on Main Street," you would spend forever trying to figure out which of the hundreds of other streets to take instead. They would be of much more help to you if they said, "Turn left at the next exit." When you know what *to do*, you have a direction. When you only know what *not to do*, you remain lost.

As you think about values, we encourage you to think about what you *want to do*, not what you *don't want to do*. Examples of *to do* goals include "Enroll in an art class. Adopt a puppy. Support my friends."

On the other hand, examples of "not to do" goals include "Don't smoke. Stop weighing myself. Don't criticize my children." Anytime you catch yourself writing "Don't, not, never, stop, quit, etc." you are setting what we call a dead man's goal. Dead men don't smoke. Dead men don't criticize their children. Dead men don't weigh themselves. So, keep in mind that if a dead man can do it, it's not a good goal. If you start to write a dead man's goal, ask yourself, "What can I *do* instead?" to reframe your *not to do* into a *to do*.

What Do You Want Your Life to Stand For?

To help you clarify your values, there are two techniques that we frequently use: a funeral meditation and an imaginary eulogy. These techniques are very powerful, and they might even scare you a little. The payoff for doing them is that they will give you a clear vision of what you want your life to stand for.

Funeral Meditation

We have adapted the funeral meditation from Dr. Steven Hayes and his colleagues (1999). As you are aware, death is inevitable. We can delay death, but we can never avoid it. Although you can't control when or how you will die, you can control how you live.

For this exercise, you should close your eyes and imagine that you are observing your own funeral. Visualize yourself in the casket. Smell the fresh flowers. See your loved ones and anyone else you want to see there. You can hear the words they speak about you, and your wisdom will let you pick and choose exactly what you want and need to hear from them. And within the next few moments, you may be ready to discover how you would like your loved ones to remember you. Listen carefully to each of them as they say the words that in your heart you most want to hear about you.

Your Eulogy: How Do You Want to Be Remembered?

After you complete the funeral meditation exercise, write down how each of your loved ones eulogized you:

Name of Person 1 _____

Relation to You _____

What Did This Person Say about You?

_____

_____

Name of Person 2 _____

Relation to You _____

What Did This Person Say about You?

_____

_____

Name of Person 3 _____

Relation to You _____

What Did This Person Say about You?

_____

_____

Name of Person 4 _____

Relation to You _____

What Did This Person Say about You?

_____

_____

_____

The list above reflects how people will remember you. In some cases, if you have not been living a valued life, you may be disappointed that they were not able to say what you wanted to hear. These eulogies reflect your values and give you an idea of what you really want your life to stand for. You may notice that several of the nine valued domains are represented.

An important question to ask yourself now is: Are you doing things to be the type of person you want to be? If not, now is the time to live the life you want and do the things that are most important to you.

You may have noticed that your weight and your looks are probably not mentioned in the eulogies. What does that mean? Perhaps it means that the goal you are working extremely hard to achieve is ultimately not going to matter much in the grand scheme of things. Each minute you spend weighing yourself, counting calories, or exercising excessively is a minute away from doing what really matters most to you.

And here is a very sobering reminder for you: No matter how perfect your body is, your body will decay when you die. When you focus on your physical appearance, you are investing in a part of life that will not survive beyond your years on this planet. When you focus on your valued directions, you leave a legacy that may live on even when you are no longer alive. Death cannot destroy the hard work you put into valued life directions. When you pursue your values, you leave a legacy behind: the child you raise, the friends you touch, the animals you nurture, the donations you give.

What Matters Most in Life?

Switching from imagined eulogies to real ones, here are examples of the legacy of women whose valued journey was cut short by anorexia. You will notice that those left behind remembered the valued lives, not their weight or their body shape. We do not intend for these examples to glamorize death. Instead, they show the importance of living a life according to your values. We hope these eulogies will inspire you to live the way you want to be remembered.

- *You were my only sister, and you were my best friend. I will always remember your bright smile. I feel that you are with me whenever I laugh because I have shared so much laughter with you. When I meet you in heaven, I want to give you a big hug, hear you laugh, and see your smile. That is how I will always remember you.*

- *Whenever I walk past your locker at school, I think of how much you meant to me. I think of you every day, and senior year is going to be difficult without you. I know you will be looking down from heaven to be with me and the rest of our class when we walk across the stage at graduation.*

- *Jenny loved music. She was first chair flute in the high school band, and she had a remarkable singing voice. She was a letter-winner on the track team, and she volunteered every year to coach at the Special Olympics. The mentally retarded children that she touched will always remember her loving compassion. She wanted to attend college to study music education. She had so much potential and so much to give to the world. It breaks my heart that she is gone.*

Each of these women began their valued journey toward friendship, education, leisure, family, and citizenship. Somewhere along the way, anorexia entered the picture and steered them off course. Yes, these women were behaving in valued ways, but behavior alone was not enough. ACT also encourages a commitment to life-enhancing values, and we will talk more about commitment in the next chapter. At some point, these women became more committed to being thin than they were to being students, friends, sisters, or productive citizens. Giving into and acting upon their strong drive to be thin by continuing to diet eventually made it no longer possible for them to pursue their love of family, and friends, and music. Anorexia had become a terminal roadblock.

Remember that valued living is a lifelong process in which road blocks and barriers arise. These women succumbed to the barrier called anorexia. They lived a valued life *and* responded to painful thoughts and anorexic urges by continuing to starve themselves. This can happen unless you learn new and more constructive ways of dealing with such feelings and urges. In the next chapter, we will discuss how anorexia can be a barrier for you and how you can deal with the anorexia barrier—so you can live a life according to your values *and give yourself a chance to complete your journey!*

Each day you live is a day to move in a valued direction and take your painful thoughts and feelings with you. In a way, we write our own eulogies by the actions that we take each and every day. Once again, what do you want your eulogy to say once you are old and gray? Please give yourself some time to think about this. It is one of the most (if not *the* most) important questions that we ask you in this workbook.

Your Timeline

Think about your life: past, present, and future. What are important events in your life? Please take a look at the timeline on the next page. Starting with your birth, include all the events that define your life. Use the timeline in the book or draw your own if you'd like more space. You can include positive events, upsetting events, or any other important things that have happened or you expect to happen to you. Use tick marks and mark the events that happened or that you expect to happen on your timeline.

This timeline represents your life. Do you notice any themes in your timeline? Which of the nine valued domains do your timeline events fit into? Some clients we have worked with have given us examples from the family domain, such as parents divorcing, sibling's birth, special holidays with family, etc. We also see clients who value achievements in education or career, such as winning an award, getting a promotion, etc.

In some cases, clients do indicate anorexia in the timeline, but anorexia is often depicted in the context of a health value, such as "Decided to seek counseling" or "Threw away my skinny clothes." Now look at the timeline and notice: where does your weight fit in? Not one client we have worked with has ever listed a weight-related achievement. Never have we seen "Reached ninety pounds" or "Finally fit into size zero jeans" written on a timeline.

Look again at your timeline. This will tell you what is most important to you.

My Life Timeline

Birth ——————————————————————————— Death

Write Your Own Epitaph

Another powerful exercise, also adapted from Hayes and his colleagues (1999), will help you clarify values. Think about the headstone on your grave. What inscription (epitaph) would you like to see on it that will capture the essence of your life and sum up the things that matter most to you?

This may seem like another strange and somewhat scary exercise. If you stick with it and complete it *and* feel a bit queasy, it will help you further clarify what you want your life to stand for. Now we want you to imagine that the headstone in the drawing is on your own grave. Notice that the epitaph has not yet been written. What inscription would you like to see on it that will capture the essence of your life? What is it that you want to be remembered for? What would you like your life to stand for?

Again, please give yourself some time to think about this really important question. If you find an answer—or a few different options—just write them all down on the lines below the drawing. You can come back to them later.

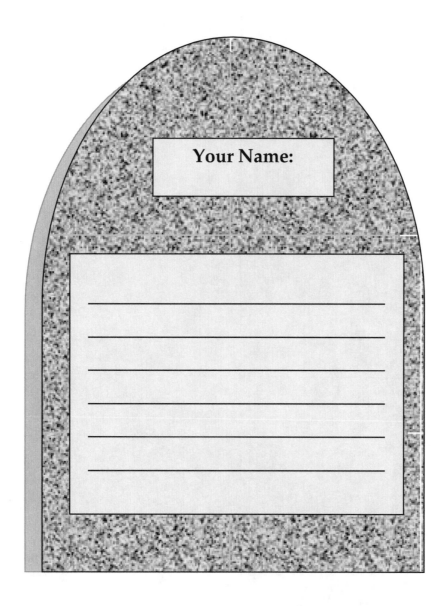

Your Name:

Values Narrative Worksheet

Now that you have explored what you want your life to stand for, write down your values in each of the domains inside the hearts on the following worksheet. To guide your narrative, consider asking yourself the following questions for each of the domains.

Family

What type of sister do you want to be? What type of parent do you want to be? How do you want to interact with your family members?

_____

_____

Friends

What type of friend do you want to be? What does it mean to be a good friend? How would you behave toward your best friend? Why is friendship important to you?

_____

_____

Romantic Relationships

What is your ideal relationship like? What kind of partner do you want to be in an intimate relationship? How would you treat your partner? What type of relationship would you like to have?

_____

_____

Leisure

What type of activities do you enjoy? What type of activities would you really like to engage in? Why do you enjoy them?

_____

_____

Citizenship

What can you do to make the world a brighter place? Are community activities (e.g., volunteering, voting, recycling) important to you? Why?

_____

_____

Spirituality

This domain does not necessarily refer to organized religion. It is about faith and spirituality. Why is faith important to you? If this is an important area in your life, what is it that makes this so important?

_____

_____

Health

Write down your values related to maintaining your physical well-being. Why do you take care of yourself? How do you take care of yourself?

_____

_____

Education

Why is learning important to you? Are there any skills you'd like to learn?

_____

_____

Career

What do you value about your career? Financial security? A career in the helping professions? Intellectual challenge? Independence? Prestige? Getting to interact with other people? What type of work would you like to do?

_____

_____

Values Assessment Worksheet

Now that you have explored each of the value domains, we would like you to complete the values assessment worksheet to identify your most important values. Based on the

Values Narrative

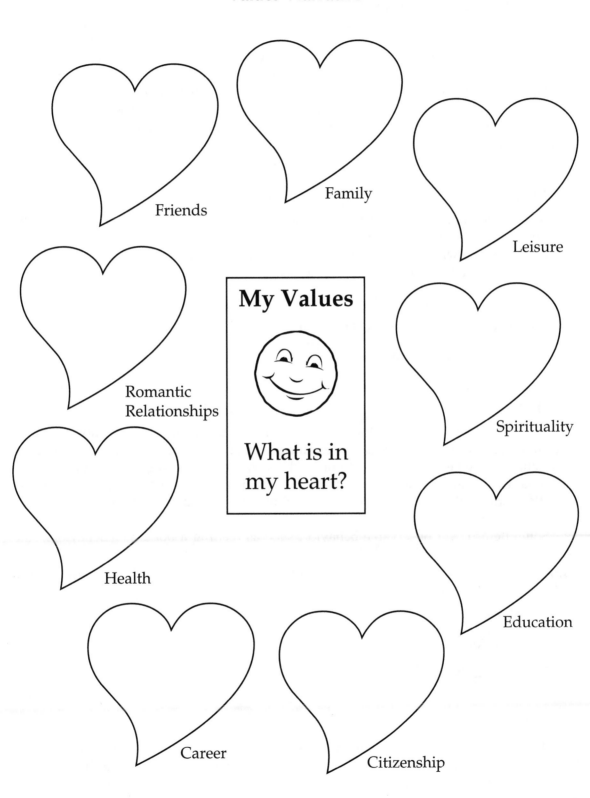

values you identified, we will then help you prepare an action plan with goals that are based on the values you identified.

The first Valued Living Questionnaire was developed by psychologist Kelly Wilson in 2002. We have constructed a Values Assessment Worksheet that is similar to a Pleasant Events Schedule (PES) Questionnaire developed by psychologist Peter Lewinsohn and his colleagues (1992). Although our items are different, the scoring structure is based on the PES.

For each of the nine values domains, we list five items that reflect values people frequently express for that domain. Below each set of five examples, there is an empty space for you to add your own personal value. First, though, we'll give you some instructions for filling in the worksheet.

Importance

In this column, please rate how important each value is to you. Please rate the importance even if you have not engaged in or experienced the valued behavior recently.

Not everyone will value all of these areas, or value all areas the same. So please rate each area according to your own personal sense of importance.

0 = This is not important to me

1 = This is moderately important to me

2 = This is very important to me

Action

In this column, please rate how often you have taken action toward moving closer to your values in the last month. These ratings will give you an idea of how consistent your actions have been with each of your values. We are not asking about your ideal in each area. We are also not asking what others think of you. Everyone does better in some areas than others. We want to know how *you* think you have been doing in these areas in the last thirty days.

Some items cover observable behavior, such as reading a book. For behaviors, rate how often you engaged in the behavior, using the scale below. Other items cover feelings, such as feeling secure. For feelings, rate how often you experienced the feeling, using the scale below.

0 = Not in the last month

1 = Occasionally in the last month

2 = Frequently in the last month

Match

Are you doing things that you value? You can find out by multiplying your importance score and your action score. For example, the first item is "helping family members." Let's say helping family is very important to you. You would put a 2 in the importance column. In terms of action, you recall that you only helped a family member twice this month. So you might put a "1" for occasional action. Your match score is 2 x 1, which equals 2.

Add to Plan

In the Plan column, place a check mark if you would like to practice this valued behavior. For example, as you think about your desire to help your family, you may decide that you would like to add helping your family to your activity plan. In that case, you can place a check mark in the "Add to Plan" column to alert you when you are ready to prepare your plan later.

The sample we've just described is listed in italics at the top of the Values Assessment Worksheet. Now, you're ready to complete the assessment yourself.

Domain	Importance (0 to 2)	Action (0 to 2)	Match (importance x consistency)	Add to Plan?
Sample:	2	1	2	✓
Family				
Helping family members				
Attending family functions				
Spending quality time with family				
Strong connection with family				
Being a good/devoted daughter				
Friends				
Sharing good and bad news with friends				
Trusting other people with my secrets				
Doing fun activities with friends				
Supporting friends who need help				
Meeting someone new				
Romantic Relationships / Marriage				
Planning a date				
Expressing affection				
Having a loving relationship				
Commitment				
Companionship				

Domain	Importance (0 to 2)	Action (0 to 2)	Match (importance x consistency)	Add to Plan?
Education				
Learning more about a topic I enjoy				
Achievement: Passing/Getting a good grade				
Solving problems				
Reading a book				
Doing activities that challenge me				
Career				
Earning a paycheck				
Doing a good job at work				
Helping others for a living				
Doing what I enjoy for a living				
Job security				
Leisure				
Having a hobby				
Participating in or watching sports				
Listening to music I like				
Doing meditation or relaxation				
Joining or participating in a club				
Spirituality				
Communing with nature				
Participating in organized religion				
Having faith				
Supporting my faith (e.g. prayer, fasting, meditation)				
Feeling connected to a higher power				

Domain	Importance (0 to 2)	Action (0 to 2)	Match (importance x consistency)	Add to Plan?
Citizenship				
Volunteering				
Educating others				
Expressing my political views				
Protecting the earth				
Feeling patriotic				
Health				
Feeling rested/Getting a good night's sleep				
Wanting to live a full life				
Taking care of my body				
Willingness to seek professional help				
Being mentally healthy				

Scoring Your Values Assessment Worksheet

In the following section we'd like to tell you more about what your scores mean in terms of how important values are to you and how much importance and action match in your life.

Importance

After you complete your ratings, you can add up your importance scores. The higher your score, the more values you were able to identify across all domains. Your importance score can range from 0 to 90 (if you only answered the items provided) or from 0 to 108 (if you included additional items).

Action

Next, add your action scores. The higher your score, the more action you have taken toward a valued life. Your action score can range from 0 to 90 (if you only answered the items provided) or from 0 to 108 (if you included additional items).

Match

Your match score will tell you how consistently your actions match your values. Are you doing things that are important to you? Your match score can range from 0 to 180 (if you only answered the items provided) or from 0 to 216 (if you included additional items). Higher scores reflect a good match between your values and your behavior.

If you find that your match score is low, there are several reasons that could explain this finding:

- *You are not doing things that are important to you.* In this case, your importance score is high, but your action score is low. This is one of the most common patterns we come across in our clinical practice. This pattern means that you have identified your values, but you are not moving in a direction that supports those values. In this case, you should plan more action-oriented valued activities into your schedule. There may be barriers that stand in your way. Chapter 7 will help you deal with those barriers.

- *You are doing things that are not important to you.* In this case, your action score is high, and your importance score is low. This pattern means that you need to re-evaluate how you spend your day. How can you plan to do more valued activities and reduce the number of less valued activities? You may also need to explore your values more and to identify your most important values.

- *You have trouble identifying values and taking action.* In this case, you have low action and low importance scores. This means that you have trouble identifying what is important to you and you have trouble taking actions that will move you in the direction of your values. If this is the case, the first step is to identify what you value. This chapter will help you to explore valued directions. After you know what you want your life to stand for, you can take action and cope with barriers that stand in your way.

Add to Plan

You can copy the calendar on pages 114 and 115 to plan your weekly activities. Schedule times to practice mindfulness exercises *and* engage in valued activities you selected from your questionnaire above.

" The journey of a thousand miles begins with one step."

—Chinese Saying

	SUNDAY	MONDAY	TUESDAY
7 A.M.			
8 A.M.			
9 A.M.			
10 A.M.			
11 A.M.			
12 noon			
1 P.M.			
2 P.M.			
3 P.M.			
4 P.M.			
5 P.M.			
6 P.M.			
7 P.M.			
8 P.M.			
9 P.M.			
10 P.M.			
11 P.M.			
12 midnight			
1 A.M.			
2 A.M.			
3 A.M.			
4 A.M.			
5 A.M.			
6 A.M.			

WEDNESDAY	THURSDAY	FRIDAY	SATURDAY

CHAPTER 8

Staying Committed to Valued Living

In this chapter you will learn to:

* Identify barriers that make valued living difficult for you

* Cope with barriers you face

* Commit to living a valued life

In the last chapter, you identified your life values and explored what you want your life to stand for. Hopefully, you have established a direction and begun taking important first steps on your journey to recovery and valued living. In this chapter, you will continue to put valuing into action and learn to cope with the situations, feelings, and other barriers that make valued living difficult for you.

When we first discuss valued directions with clients, we often hear several *"yes ... but"* responses.

* *"Yes*, I value volunteering, *but* I don't have time."

* *"Yes,* I want to be a better spouse, *but* my parents weren't ideal models of healthy relationships."

* *"Yes,* spirituality is important to me, *but* I don't like the people at my church."

Now is the time to get off your *but(t)* and start living a valued life. Remember what we said in chapter 3? Yes-butting keeps you stuck where you are. This is what we meant in chapter 3 when we talked about how powerful language can be and how destructive it can be at times. Yes-butting can trap us into corners and keep us from moving forward.

In this chapter, we will give you a number of examples of how you can replace your "yes-buts" with the word "and." Such simple and seemingly subtle changes in language and behavior can make a big difference in helping you move toward your valued ends, where you truly want to go.

So, in this chapter, we'll teach you how to act on your values even as you face barriers that complicate valued living. We'll start off with a case example of a client who gave a "yes . . . but" response to valued living, and we'll describe how she coped with her barriers. After you read her story, we will ask you to examine your own barriers and prepare a plan to deal with some of the bumps you may encounter on your own journey.

Jasmine's Struggle to Live a Valued Life

Jasmine, a telemarketer, dropped out of college more than 10 years ago because she was unable to make up work she missed following her hospitalization for anorexia. Recently, Jasmine experienced a relapse of anorexia and entered ACT treatment with us.

When we discussed career values in treatment, Jasmine described her childhood dream of becoming a schoolteacher. Jasmine fondly recalled a special Christmas when Santa brought her a chalkboard set, and she played teacher every day. She positioned her dolls in rows in front of the chalkboard, and she presented lessons on adding, reading, and spelling. She even prepared an attendance book to take roll.

Now, at age thirty-one, whenever Jasmine thought about being a teacher, she did not recall the happy memories of her childhood. Instead, she thought about all the excuses as to why teaching was not possible. Yes, she wanted to return to school to be a teacher, BUT . . .

- There won't be enough time to study.

- She's an "old lady" and she won't fit in with all of the young kids in college.

- How could she afford to cut back on the hours at work to attend college?

- If she had to drop out again, she'd be an even bigger loser than she already is.

- The economy is so bad, there aren't many teaching job openings these days.

Like Jasmine, perhaps you have given up on your childhood dreams. Think about the dreams you had when you were young. Are you currently living the life that you dreamed about as a child? If not, what excuses and "yes-buts" are standing in your way?

1._____

2._____

3._____

In the next exercise, you will explore your personal barriers to valued living in greater depth. For now, just recognize that, like Jasmine, you probably face barriers that currently prevent you from moving in the valued directions that you identified in the last chapter. Perhaps your barriers are similar to Jasmine's barriers, such as time constraints, financial cost and risks, and fear of failure. Jasmine decided those barriers were too much, and working toward being a schoolteacher was too difficult and risky and just not worth it!

In therapy, we asked Jasmine to take a minute and close her eyes, imagining that little girl with her attendance book and chalkboard. Then we asked her to think about that little girl's love of teaching. Is that little girl worth it? Was Jasmine willing to commit to making that little girl's dream come true? Jasmine became teary and agreed that the answer was clearly, "Yes, that little girl is worth it. I'll do it for her."

Over the next few months, Jasmine worked to accommodate the barriers she faced. She cut back her work hours from forty to twenty-four hours per week to allow time to enroll in two college courses for her education degree. She applied for and earned a small grant to fund her tuition, and she asked her family to help her pay the remaining costs. She saved additional money by getting rid of her cable television and selling her car to buy a less expensive model. Jasmine was also willing to risk the embarrassment and failure of returning to school.

Obviously, it was not easy for Jasmine to make sacrifices and take emotional risks to pursue her career value. Valued living is not meant to be easy. If it were easy, we would all be living valued lives. Valued living is about commitment. It is a test of your integrity.

Commitment means getting up when you are down and facing barriers you encounter on your journey. The next time you watch the Olympics, notice when the gold medalist cries on the award podium. You will see that those tears represent not just the joy of success but also the sacrifice, pain, and risk that went into the endeavor of elite athletics.

Also, Jasmine was right in bringing up the issue of risk. It is undoubtedly risky to make a change. Things can and sometimes do go wrong. Perhaps she will indeed fail her first exam in one of her courses. Perhaps she will fall asleep with her book in her hands because she is so exhausted. Perhaps she will not find a teaching job right away. These are all valid thoughts and considerations.

However, the biggest risk for Jasmine is not taking a risk at all. You may wonder why that is the biggest risk. The answer is very simple: If you don't take any risk, if you want to play it super safe, nothing will change. You can count on that. And if nothing changes, you will definitely go where you are headed now. Is that the place where your values are? Is that where you truly want to go?

What Barriers Do You Face?

In this section we would like you to think about each of your valued directions and consider what stands in the way of pursuing each direction. You can refer to your worksheets in chapter 7 to review your values statements and then list barriers to those values in the worksheet below.

Barriers-to-Values Worksheet

Family

    Values Statement: _____

    Barriers: _____

Friends

    Values Statement: _____

    Barriers: _____

Romantic Relationships

Values Statement: _____

Barriers: _____

Leisure

Values Statement: _____

Barriers: _____

Citizenship

Values Statement: _____

Barriers: _____

Spirituality

Values Statement: _____

Barriers: _____

Health

Values Statement: _____

Barriers: _____

Education

Values Statement: _____

Barriers: _____

Career

Values Statement: _____

Barriers: _____

Types of Barriers

Below is a list of common barriers people face. We will review each one of the barriers and suggest ways for you to accept them and carry them with you on your valued journey.

- I don't have any values!

- Notice if evaluations prevent you from moving

- Thoughts and feelings that steer you off course

- Social pressure to abandon values: What will other people think?

- Is it really your value?

- The anorexia barrier

1. I Don't Have Any Values!

Some clients we treat say they don't value anything. What they actually mean to say is that they feel too helpless and afraid to express their values. They do in fact have values. Sometimes caring hurts, especially if the value you care about has been a source of suffering.

Take the example of Gail, who said, "I don't necessarily value being part of a loving family because I don't even know what a loving family is all about. Every time I try to reach out to a family member, they just push me away. My family is so dysfunctional that there is no point in me even thinking about family values."

On the one hand, Gail said that she does not value family. On the other hand, she mentioned that she reaches out to her family (and cares!) To help Gail out of this apparent dilemma, we asked her to reframe the way she identified her values. Instead of asking herself, "Can I *achieve* this?" we recommended she ask herself, "Do I *care about* this?"

Remember that values are different from goals. Gail was thinking in terms of goals and achievements. She was correct that there was no point in setting the impossible goal of having the most loving family on Earth. However, she could certainly say that she cared about her family. She could behave in ways that support her value of family, with the knowledge that her family's dysfunction might not yield the loving outcome that she desired.

Remember that values are not about achieving outcomes. As you learned in chapter 7, values are lifelong journeys, in which you may or may not reach certain destinations. The point of valuing is that you do your part, and you do what is most important to you in life. You may or may not achieve desired outcomes.

If you are like Gail and say, "I don't have values," start asking yourself, "Do I care about this?" If you still have trouble identifying values, think back to a time when you were younger, before you encountered any pain on your valued direction. What did that child inside of you care about? It is quite likely that the values that come into your mind from back then are at least some of the ones that you still care about now.

2. Notice if Evaluations Prevent You from Moving

Some people complete the values assessment in chapter 7 and easily identify what they want their life to stand for. Their gut reaction is often, "Yes! Yes! Yes! I value parenting, friendship, communing with nature, education, etc." Then problems arise when people begin to doubt and question their values. Do I have enough money? Do I have enough time? Am I too stupid to do this? What would my friends think if I chose this?

These evaluations cause people to second-guess themselves and wonder if they truly hold their chosen values. If you find yourself doing this, remember what you learned about acceptance in chapter 5. Acceptance is about not judging your thoughts as "good" or "bad." Now it is time to apply a nonjudgmental perspective to values. There is no such thing as a good value or a bad value. Go with your gut reaction and choose without judging.

To further explain the concept of choosing, we use an example described by Eugene Herrigel (1953) in the book *Zen in the Art of Archery*. He described how animals and infants reach for objects without hesitation. However, adults, who have the ability to evaluate their choices, often hesitate before reaching for an object. They debate whether or not they really want to reach for an object. Observe your surroundings and you will notice this too. Learn from babies and animals, and choose to act without hesitation.

3. Thoughts and Feelings That Steer You Off Course

How can you cope with self-doubt that discourages valuing? Just remember the "Take Your Mind For a Walk" exercise you learned in chapter 5. This exercise was your opportunity to practice moving in your own direction, even if you experienced unwanted thoughts that tried to steer you off course.

A similar technique is the bus driver metaphor, that was originally described by Steven Hayes and his colleagues (1999). We have adopted this metaphor for the purposes of this workbook to make it applicable to anorexia. Imagine yourself as a bus driver. Along your route, you pick up some unruly passengers, which we liken to the unwanted thoughts and feelings that your mind serves up for you. These passengers intimidate you as you drive along your chosen route. They taunt you with statements such as, "This route has too much traffic," "Turn left here," and "Stop this bus right now." In essence, the passengers want you to change your direction and take another route, a route that they have chosen, not the route you want to take.

Think about the passengers that Jasmine picked up as she drove her bus in the school-teacher direction. She was escorting some unruly passengers that taunted her with, "You failed before," "There are no teaching jobs out there anyway," and "You don't have time or money." What passengers are you carrying on your own bus? Like Jasmine, are you letting those thoughts steer you in the opposite direction of where you want to go? Are you like the three women whose eulogies we presented in the previous chapter? They were driving the bus on the valued route. Then they picked up passengers that said, "Diet. Diet. Diet. You're not thin enough yet." The passengers took control and drove off to the anorexia dead end—literally. ACT says, "Let those passengers yell while you stay committed to your life-enhancing values!"

Remember that *you* are the driver. Your hands, not the words of the passengers, steer that bus. Words alone cannot take you off course. As you learned in chapter 5, thoughts are just words and words are just sounds. Just listen to the passengers' taunts. Stay on the valued route, whatever the passengers might say to you. With ACT, you can let those passengers yell as you stay commited.

Eventually, the passengers will learn that they cannot distract you from your route, no matter what they say. They may be unruly at first, and they may even get louder when you don't do as they say. Eventually, however, they will leave you alone if you continue to drive, as you choose. Drive and act in a valued direction. Let your values drive your behavior, not your thoughts. Let your values guide you through your life, not your thoughts.

Remember that thoughts and feelings come and go. In contrast, behavior cannot be erased that easily. There may be times when you carry passengers on your bus that try to convince you that you "don't feel like doing this anymore" or "you're never going to succeed anyway." Even if you start to think about giving up on a valued direction, continue moving. The effects of behavior are more permanent. Hard work won't disappear, and the progress you make will be for real and won't just go away. This is what really matters. Ultimately you are in control of the direction of your life bus—you do it with your hands and feet. And the fact that you have that kind of control and power is really great news indeed!

The bus driver metaphor is a great reminder that *you* really are in control of your destination. When we discussed in chapter 4 what you can and cannot control in your life, we talked a lot about how you cannot control the way you think and feel about yourself through dieting. The bus driver metaphor illustrates once again that you can't control what passenger thoughts and feelings will ride along with you. Yet this metaphor also shows you what happens if you control what you can control: the steering wheel with your hands, the accelerator with your feet. You control what you do with your hands and feet. You will go where you let your hands and feet take you—*that* is what you truly can control.

4. Social Pressure to Abandon Values: What Will Other People Think?

Sometimes we are reluctant to live a valued life because we evaluate our values and decide that we are "not smart enough," "not attractive enough," or "not worthy enough." In other situations, these discouragement barriers come from other people in our lives. Think about important people in your life. Has anyone made comments that discourage you from pursuing a certain valued direction? List below the discouraging comments other people have expressed to you:

1. _____

2. _____

3. _____

Now, take some comfort in knowing that you are not the only person who has faced social pressure to abandon a valued choice. The history books are filled with examples of people who moved in chosen directions, even as they faced social pressure to abandon those directions.

One of the most prominent examples is Christopher Columbus. He valued discovery and adventure, and he chose to sail a Western route from Spain to India. As you know from the history textbooks, the popular opinion at that time was that the world was flat. People judged Columbus a fool, destined to sail off the face of the earth. Columbus did not allow these people and their comments to steer him off his course. He chose to follow through with his value instead of conceding to the judgments of others.

Imagine if Columbus did a "yes-but" and said, "Yes, I want to discover this new route, but I might die and people will laugh at me." What would have happened?

1. He would not have made an amazing discovery.

2. He could only wonder what would have really happened if he had followed through with his plans. He would have spent his life dreaming away without experiencing his values.

Now think about your own life. You are faced with a similar choice as Columbus. You can follow through with your valued choices *or* you can give in to social pressure to abandon the life you want to lead, never discovering and never experiencing.

Which option do you want to choose? Please make a check mark next to your choice.

❑ I am going to give in to the detractors and hesitate on valued living.

❑ I am committed to this valued direction, and I am going to keep moving.

5. Is It Really Your Value?

Just as social pressure can lead us to abandon our chosen values, social pressure can also lead us to identify values that we don't really own. When people complete the value identification, they sometimes choose values that sound socially appropriate or values that their loved ones expect of them.

For example, when we discussed education values, Jackie described her experience as a first-year law student. It soon became apparent that she was miserable in school, and she had no desire for a career in law. She only entered law school to make her parents happy. We worked with Jackie to explore more valued career options, and she eventually chose massage therapy. Jackie did value having a good relationship with her parents, and we discussed alternative ways for Jackie to honor her parents without giving up on her other values that were important to her.

Be sure that your values are *your* values, not values that society, friends, or family impose on you. Ask yourself: Why am I doing this? Am I doing this for me or for someone else?

Remember that the pursuit of values is about discovering or rediscovering your own life. It's time to put yourself first! If you are familiar with air travel, you know the standard safety instruction: "When the oxygen masks come down, *put your mask on first* before attending to others." (We thank Dr. Jeannie Sperry for this example).

6. The Anorexia Barrier

There is a Buddhist saying, "If you don't decide where you are going, you will end up where you are headed." Values can prevent you from heading toward a gloomy, potentially fatal destination called anorexia. Many clients recognize the cost of having anorexia when they discuss their values. Here are some typical statements we have heard:

- Casey, twenty-seven, Nascar fan: *Anorexia is an all-consuming, around-the-clock job. I don't have friends anymore because I have no room for other people in my life. People stopped inviting me out, because they know I avoid social gatherings that involve food. Even if there is no food involved, I usually can't go out because I am so tired when I'm done exercising that I don't want to do anything but sleep.*

- Wanda, fifteen, gymnast: *I started gymnastics when I was five, and I love to feel like I'm flying in the air. Unfortunately, I can't train now because my coach kicked me out of the gym again because of my eating disorder. She said I could not come back until I started eating. They were also worried about my health because I had too many stress fractures. I don't understand the connection exactly, but they said my bones were too weak because I stopped getting my period.*

- Grace, nineteen, former Girl Scout: *I feel so bad for my parents. I know my mom cries at night because she is scared I will die. I cry for her too. I never wanted to hurt my family or worry them. I'm so sorry. I love my parents so much.*

From these examples, you can see how high the cost of dieting has been for these young women in the valued domains of friends (Casey), leisure (Wanda and Casey), health (Wanda), and family (Grace).

Now think about your own life. Before starting to work with this book, you may have thought for a long time that there was no greater value than being a slim person who feels good about herself. You may have wondered if you would ever become the person you want to be *unless* you continue to diet and lose more and more weight.

At this point, after completing the values exercises, this belief may have started to crumble and you may begin to wonder if you will ever become the person you want to be *if* you continue to diet and lose more and more weight. At this point, you may have started to realize that every minute you spend counting calories is a minute that you aren't devoting to other values.

It is very important that you are very clear about this and fully understand the ways dieting interferes with your valued living. For this reason, we ask you to list below the ways dieting interferes with your pursuit of valued directions.

1. _____

2. _____

3. _____

4. _____

Traveling with Your Fears

If want to live a valued life, you may have to change your behavior and give up dieting. In the book *Hope for the Flowers* (1972), author Trina Paulus writes, "How exactly does one become a butterfly? You must want to fly so badly that you are willing to give up being a caterpillar."

Are you ready to change? Do you want to fly so badly that you are willing to eat food to have the strength to pursue your valued directions? If so, we recommend you contact a nutritionist. Most hospitals employ a nutritionist, and you can call your local hospital to schedule an appointment with a nutritionist who has worked with people with anorexia. A nutritionist will design a meal plan to meet your nutrition needs. You can read chapter 11 for more details about that aspect of treatment.

Again, we do not want to set any eating or weight-gain goals for you. Our only concern is for you to eat and weigh enough to keep you as strong and healthy as is necessary to live the life you want to live.

If you are not ready to change, you might be thinking, "Hold on! Eating will trigger my fears and cause me to freak out." If you are concerned about the thoughts and feelings you will experience when you eat, we recommend that you practice the mindfulness and acceptance exercises you learned in chapters 5 and 6. Experience your thoughts and feelings and allow them to come and go. You can learn to travel with your fears on your journey toward valued living.

Bear Your Cross

We'll give you a case example of Anya, a client who carried her fears and anorexia with her on her valued journey. She is a good example of someone who moved in her valued directions *and* had a number of fearful thoughts while doing so.

When discussing spiritual values, Anya pointed to a cross-shaped necklace she wore, and she described how she believed anorexia was her "cross to bear." She explained that she believes God assigns suffering to each of us, and anorexia was her designated burden. The anorexia cross was heavy to bear, and her anorexia symptoms often slowed her progress toward valued directions.

Ultimately, Anya vowed to bear her cross and to move, and keep on moving, in valued directions. When she wanted to go the beach with her cousin, she took her fear of being seen publicly in a bathing suit with her. When her parents took her to dinner, Anya ate her meal and observed her thoughts of wanting to vomit. She ate *and* bore her uncomfortable thoughts.

You obviously do not need to share Anya's spiritual belief to appreciate the metaphorical value of her explanation. You too can move in a valued direction and bear the cross of anorexia. The verb "to bear" is defined in Roget's Dictionary as "to carry, to suffer, to produce, to have." This definition hits the nail on the head. If you choose *to carry* your anorexic fears in a valued direction, you may *suffer, and* you will also *produce* valued behavior, which will allow you *to have* a life filled with valued rewards.

We want to make sure that you really grasp the significance of this rather long and important sentence. So we will repeat it one more time for you: If you choose *to carry* your anorexic fears in a valued direction, you may *suffer, and* you will also *produce* valued behavior, which will allow you *to have* a life filled with valued rewards.

Anya wore the gold-cross necklace to remind herself to carry the burden of anorexia with her as she moved in her valued directions. Like Anya, you may want to have a motivational reminder of your commitment to valued directions.

Another client we worked with put a photo her family on the refrigerator to remind herself that eating improves her relationship with her family. When she eats in a more healthy way, there is more harmony at home and she argues less with her family about food.

What kind of reminder object would motivate you to carry the burden of anorexia *and* remain committed to your valued directions? List your idea below:

_____

You Can Do It Too!

Is it really possible to move in a valued direction if your life is filled with setbacks and disappointments? To answer that question, we want you to think about what you remember about Abraham Lincoln. List the three most important facts you know about Lincoln:

1. _____

2. _____

3. _____

Most people remember Lincoln as a good president, the man who freed the slaves, the writer of the inspirational Gettysburg Address. His accomplishments truly stand out. Even almost 140 years after his death, most Americans would be able to write a brief epitaph for him if they were asked to do so.

That is why it may surprise you to know that Lincoln bore many crosses on his way to the White House. In fact, much of his early life reads like a story about a loser. Lincoln was born in poverty. He had little formal schooling. His family was too poor for him to attend school, and Lincoln had to educate himself to pursue his value of education.

When he was nine years old, his mother died. He also witnessed all of his other siblings die premature deaths. The first woman he asked to marry him rejected his proposal. He eventually did get married and fathered four sons. He buried two of them. Professionally, Lincoln entered his first political race for a county legislative seat, and lost. He then opened a business, which failed and left Lincoln in debt. If you have seen pictures of Lincoln, you also probably noticed that he was not a very attractive man. He once quipped, "If I was two-faced, would I be wearing this one?"

Obviously, Lincoln faced many barriers: poverty, grief, failure, rejection, unattractiveness. He could have easily "yes-butted" himself out of history. "Yes, I value citizenship, but I already lost one election. There's no point in running again." What is most extraordinary about Lincoln is the fact that none of the obstacles he faced defined his life. He is not remembered as "the guy with the ugly face" or "the guy overcome with bereavement." Instead, valued directions, like citizenship, define his life. That is what he is remembered for.

You can do it too! We sometimes recommend that clients carry a penny with them. The penny bears the image of Lincoln, and it can serve as a reminder that you too can lead a valued life, even with the barriers that you face. You can look at the unattractive image on the penny and carry Lincoln's unattractiveness, just as you carry your own feelings of unattractiveness on your valued journey. As Lincoln once said, "In the end, it's not the years in your life that count. It's the life in your years." Make the most of your life in the years you have.

Now, we make no promises that people will also build a Lincoln-type memorial for you at the end of your life. Yet if you persistently move in your valued directions, chances are good that you will be remembered as more than "the woman who managed to keep her weight down" or "the girl who never weighed more than ninety pounds."

What you will be remembered for—what defines your life—is up to you. It depends on what you do now. It depends on the actions you take that are consistent with your values. In this way, you can determine the wording of your own epitaph.

Now that you have identified your values, plan to stay committed to moving in valued directions and carry any barriers with you as you continue to move forward. As a sign of your commitment, we invite you to complete your "Declaration of Independence" that states your values, acknowledges barriers, and finishes with your commitment to keep moving in your valued directions.

VALUES: MY DECLARATION OF INDEPENDENCE

I, _____ , have identified what I want my life to stand for. In the pursuit of these values, I expect to encounter the following barriers:

_____

_____

_____

_____

_____

- I will carry these barriers with me as I move in my valued directions.

- I will mindfully observe thoughts and feelings on my journey.

- I will take emotional risks on my journey.

- I will eat in a healthy way so that I have the energy necessary to move in my valued directions.

I understand that I am a valuable human being who deserves the unalienable rights of life, liberty and the pursuit of happiness.

_____   _____
         Signed   Date

CHAPTER 9[*]

Emily's Journey to Recovery

In this chapter you will learn:

* About a client who recovered from anorexia through ACT

* To review your new ACT skills

* That you can recover too

Throughout this workbook, we have included various "voices of anorexia" to reflect the thoughts and feelings of clients we treat. Although the examples we have provided are based on our knowledge and experience, we also have used some fictitious examples. This chapter is different. You will now read about the real-life case of Emily (as in other cases, we changed her name to protect her anonymity).

Emily was one of the first clients we treated for anorexia using the ACT treatment approach. Emily's case demonstrates ACT in action. Emily is a great example of how you too can recover from anorexia by using the skills you have learned in the previous chapters. Before we tell you about Emily, we want to stress that no single case example can perfectly summarize the application of ACT to anorexia. Every person is unique and different. Depending on the client, we may emphasize some techniques more than others.

You may notice some aspects of this case that remind you of yourself and other aspects that don't. Your road to recovery may be quite different from Emily's. Use this chapter to practice being an *observer* of Emily's life, and don't feel your own story must

---

[*]   Some of the information and figures included in this chapter were previously published in an article by Heffner, Sperry, Eifert, & Detweiler 2002. Copyright (2002) by the Association for the Advancement of Behavior Therapy. Reprinted by permission of the publisher.

be identical to what you read. We do hope the case of Emily inspires you to heal your own suffering. Just as it did for Emily, ACT can work for you too.

We first reported Emily's story in a professional journal to educate other psychologists about how ACT can be used to help clients with anorexia (Heffner et al. 2002). We now want to share Emily's story with you. This is the journey to recovery of a young woman who valued helping others, and she would be touched to know that her story is reaching out to help you.

Emily's Story

Emily was a teenager. When she entered high school, she noticed how thin and attractive her female classmates were. They seemed to have it all. When Emily looked at her own body in the mirror, she was disgusted. How could she compare? Emily wanted to be beautiful and attractive just like her classmates.

At first, she decided to cut just a few calories. Soon, that was not enough anymore. She needed to diet more and cut out a whole meal each day. When that was not enough, she refused to eat anything for a whole day, at least once a week. Soon, that was not enough either. She designed competitions to see how many days in a row she could go without eating.

As time went on, the goal weight she desired became lower and lower. At first, Emily only planned to diet until she reached 115 pounds. When she reached 115, which was her weight when we first met her, she was not satisfied, and strove for 100 pounds. She also indicated that her "ideal" weight was even lower and closer to 90 pounds. She realized that even if she ever reached 90 pounds, it might still not be low enough. To her dismay, Emily noticed that the bar might continue to move lower and lower.

At school, Emily participated in athletics. Her swim coach began to notice that she was getting thinner and thinner. The coach threatened to kick Emily off the team if she didn't maintain her weight and eat more. He required her to keep a food diary to detail what she ate. Metaphorically speaking, Emily wanted to have her cake and eat it too: She wanted to compete and she wanted to diet at the same time. To solve this problem, Emily lied in her food diary to make it look like she was eating more than she actually did.

Emily's mom began to worry about her too. She was concerned that Emily was getting thinner and was frightened by what the steady weight loss might do to her daughter's health and well-being. Emily never ate breakfast. She told her mother she was too busy or too tired to eat in the morning. To stop her mom from nagging, Emily often agreed to eat a granola bar, fruit, or other snack on the way to school. Emily always put the snack in her backpack and then threw it away at school instead of eating it.

When Emily stopped getting her menstrual period, her mother took Emily to see the family physician. Emily downplayed her symptoms and told the doctor her mom was just over-reacting. The doctor, who specialized in *medical* problems, did not recognize the severity of Emily's *psychological* symptoms. The doctor bought into Emily's denial and told Emily's mom that dieting was normal for teenage girls. Mom, however, knew better and realized that her daughter's denial and self-starvation were serious problems.

At that point, Emily's mom called our clinic, and Emily and her mother arrived for their first appointment. During our first session, Emily gave several reasons to convince us why she did not need to participate in therapy.

"I don't diet that much. I'm not that bad."

"My parents can't afford to pay for sessions."

"Psychologists are quacks who can't help people anyway."

Does Emily Have Anorexia?

Emily denied that she had a problem and believed she did not need help. What do you think? Does Emily have anorexia? You may want to review the symptoms of anorexia in chapter 1 to make your decision. Here is what we learned about Emily from the initial interview:

1. Emily's body weight was extremely low. Her body mass index, as you calculated in chapter 1, was less than 18.

2. Emily rigidly controlled how much she ate, often refusing to eat for days at a time. She often wrote herself notes, such as "Don't be a whale," to motivate her dieting.

3. Emily feared weight gain. She weighed herself repeatedly throughout the day to ensure that she had not gained weight.

4. Emily's menstrual period had stopped for more than three months.

5. Other than excessive dieting, Emily did not do anything else to control her weight. For instance, she did not vomit or use laxatives.

What is your diagnosis for Emily? _____

After we interviewed Emily and her mother, we considered the eating disorder diagnostic options that you learned about in chapter 1. Emily displayed all of the symptoms that professionals have established for the diagnosis of anorexia, restricting type. However, as we discussed in chapter 1, there are more important issues than coming up with the correct diagnosis, because diagnostic systems change all the time and are mainly a way for professionals to summarize the problems of a particular client such as Emily.

We were less concerned with whether Emily displayed every single symptom of anorexia and more concerned with Emily's poor quality of life. Dieting consumed her life. She was nearly kicked off her athletic team, she fought with her family about eating, and she was too weak and tired to participate in activities she used to enjoy. We wanted Emily to reclaim her life! It was time for her to ACT.

Treating Emily with ACT

We wanted to help Emily. However, we were concerned that our weekly outpatient clinic may not provide the intensive services that Emily might require to deal with her substantial problems. We thought about referring Emily to a more intensive inpatient eating disorder treatment program available in certain hospitals and clinics.

We discussed this option with Emily and her mother. Her mother requested that we treat Emily and refer her out only if she did not improve. Emily had no strong opinion about these treatment options, because she basically didn't want to participate in any form of treatment at all. Eventually we all agreed that we would work with Emily for four weeks, and then review her progress to determine if she was benefiting from our treatment program.

Preparing for Treatment

Before we began treatment, we spent time with Emily to help her prepare for therapy. Emily was a pleasant young woman, and she was easy to talk to. We talked about her fear that treatment would force her to eat and gain weight. We made it clear that we would not teach her to stop dieting. Instead, we would teach her to start living.

We saw Emily for fourteen consecutive weeks. After that we had three once-a-month follow-up sessions. So her entire treatment lasted approximately seven months.

At this point, we started to talk about Emily the person, not Emily the anorexic. Emily enjoyed writing. She had a best friend. She fed stray cats in her neighborhood. She also liked to swim, tease her younger brother, and shop at the mall. As you can see, Emily really was not much different from other teenagers attending high school.

We complimented Emily on her talents and told her that we really wanted to work with her to help make the most of her life. Emily agreed that she would give treatment a try.

Emily participated in many of the ACT treatment techniques that you have already completed in this workbook. As we summarize her treatment, you can review the techniques that you also experienced. You may even want to go back to some of them and do them again for yourself.

The Problem of Weight Control

One of the first things we did was to ask Emily to complete the "Your Reasons for Dieting" worksheet—the same worksheet you completed in chapter 4. Then we discussed the reasons Emily stated on that worksheet.

She mentioned that she wanted to be thin to be socially accepted, and she felt good when she succeeded at controlling how much she ate. She described dieting as a competition or game, in which she felt a sense of victory when she kept to her calorie limit or met her weight goal.

Emily also completed the "Coping Style Questionnaire," the same questionnaire you completed in chapter 4. Her score showed that she used control strategies in a counterproductive way. Dieting to lose weight was *the* main strategy Emily used to gain control over what and how she felt about herself.

To help explain to Emily why this strategy is flawed, and actually worked against her, we provided her with a Chinese finger trap, as described in chapter 4. Emily stuck her index fingers in at each end and tried to escape by pulling out. Of course, her fingers got stuck tighter and she experienced more discomfort. We discussed how sometimes our instinctive logical solutions to problems turn out to be no solutions at all and can actually make problems worse.

We discussed how Emily's use of dieting to feel in control or victorious was making her life more and more out of control. The more she tried to control how she looked and felt about herself through dieting, the less actual control she seemed to have over the course of her life and where she was headed. Just like in the finger trap, her wiggle room became smaller rather than larger. She knew her life was consumed by dieting.

Emily talked about how she began with a simple diet that snowballed into days of starvation. Sometimes, she felt like dieting was controlling her. Each time she met a weight goal, it was not low enough, and she needed to diet more. When would she be able to stop? Would she be able to stop at all? The answer to those two questions frightened her. We gave Emily the finger trap to take home as a reminder of the problem of control.

Acceptance

Emily learned some of the mindfulness and acceptance techniques that you practiced in chapters 5 and 6. Her first homework assignment involved thought and behavior recording. We asked Emily to write down thoughts that bothered her and rate from 0 to 10 how willing she was to experience each thought, allowing the thought to occur without reacting to it. Finally, she recorded her behavior and reactions to her thoughts. The homework sheet we provided to her looked similar to this:

Thought	Willingness to Experience Thought (0= Not Willing, 10 = Totally Willing)	Reaction/Behavior
"My stomach is gross"	*1*	*Skipped lunch*
"I'll explode if I eat that pizza"	*4*	*Removed cheese; ate some*

Emily completed her homework, and we discussed what she had discovered about herself in doing the assignment. Her record showed that when she was less willing to accept her thoughts, she dieted more. When she allowed herself to observe thoughts and let them pass, she had less need to diet. Discovering this relationship was important for Emily because it made her realize what accepting her thoughts and feelings might do for her.

We introduced the observer perspective to Emily and taught her to practice mindfulness meditation. She sat in a big, fluffy cushioned chair in our clinic, closed her eyes, and observed a thought parade. She imagined marchers carrying signs that represented the thoughts she experienced: "I'm a whale," "My stomach is gross," and any other thoughts that came to mind. Emily had a great imagination, and she clearly visualized the parade scene, from the sunny sky to the outfits the marchers wore. We provided Emily with an audiotape recording of the thought parade instructions so she could also practice this meditation at home.

When Emily returned the following week, we worked on accepting thoughts and feelings that arise in difficult situations. We asked Emily to list situations that were tough for her, using the same staircase approach that we asked you to practice in chapter 6. Her least feared situation was eating in front of other people. At the next session, Emily and the therapist ate fast-food burgers and french fries together.

As you may notice, we didn't just ask Emily to eat a little bit of low-calorie food with the therapist. Instead, we chose some foods that Emily really disliked due to their high fat content. Our intention was to bring out a lot of distressing thoughts to give Emily a good opportunity to learn to observe thoughts and feelings. You can see below that our strategy worked because Emily experienced a number of thoughts and intense feelings:

- "I might break this chair if I keep eating all this food."

- "It's so gross and disgusting. I can feel all the fat just sitting in my stomach."

At first, we asked Emily to express her thoughts and feelings out loud. Her task was simply to observe what she thought and felt and not to dismiss, argue with, or hold onto any of these thoughts and feelings.

One hour later, Emily reported that her thoughts and feelings had become less intense. She had ridden the wave of discomfort and survived. The chair did not break, and she did not crash through the floor to the room below. The nasty feeling in her stomach had passed.

For the next few weeks, Emily continued to experience uncomfortable situations on her list by riding the wave of discomfort and observing her reactions without doing anything to change her experience.

Commitment to Valued Action

We presented Emily with the bus driver metaphor, described in chapter 8. Emily now recognized the taunts of anorexia that were steering her off course. For example, Emily valued:

- A relationship with her mother, but she lied to her mother about how much she ate.

- Being a competitive swimmer, but her lap times were poor because she lost muscle mass and felt weak.

- Being a mother someday, but the absence of her menstrual period jeopardized her reproductive health.

- Being a good student, but instead of taking notes on the lecture, she used class time to write notes to herself as reminders to not eat.

The anorexia barrier, described in chapter 8, was apparent. We created a road map that we presented to Emily. As you can see, one road labeled "Dead End" represents the path of anorexia. The other road represents valued living, and it includes the valued life domains. Each domain is never-ending, to symbolize the lifelong journey of valued living. Also note that each domain is interconnected to symbolize that values domains often relate to each other. For example, you may meet new friends, as you attend college to pursue an education value, which could lead to a valued career.

Emily completed a Bus Driver homework assignment. As the driver of the bus, Emily needed to continue in her valued direction without attempting to intervene with the passengers or react to them. As homework, we asked Emily to plot a bus on a graph each day to indicate which direction she was moving her bus that day. She wrote in a daily journal about which direction she chose to take for the day. Where was her bus moving? Was she reacting to the taunts of the anorexia passengers or staying focused on her chosen route?

To help Emily clarify her values further, she completed the Funeral Meditation exercise you completed in chapter 7. She visualized the scene, and heard her parents joking about the fun-loving daughter she was. She heard her coach remembering her as a talented swimmer. Her friends remembered the good times they shared at school. Her teachers remembered her as a skilled writer. The stray cats she fed remembered how loving she was.

This exercise was a powerful reminder to Emily that she was more than a number on a scale, and that people accepted her for more than her weight and appearance. As

> *If you don't decide
> where you're going,
> you're bound to end up
> where you're headed.*
>
> —Chinese Saying

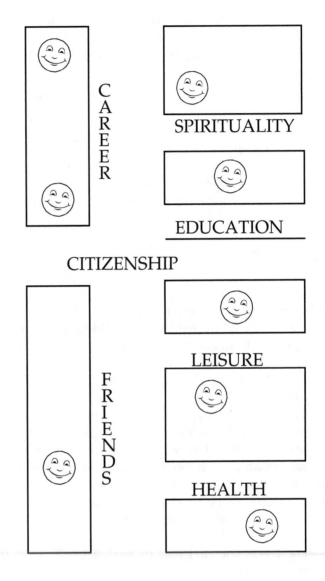

CAREER

SPIRITUALITY

EDUCATION

CITIZENSHIP

FRIENDS

LEISURE

HEALTH

FAMILY RELATIONS

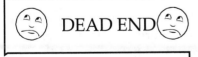 DEAD END

soon as Emily completed the funeral meditation, she asked, "What exactly do I need to eat?" It was the first time in therapy that she had expressed any interest in eating. She committed to eating breakfast each day.

The following diary entry reflects Emily's new valued direction—focus on life goals other than losing weight:

> *Each day that I live, I want to be a day to give the best of me. As of now, I am still occupied perfecting my grades, my relationship with my friends, and so on. I want to be remembered as an excellent writer. I, personally, strive to be the best in almost any area. It's not about being Miss Goody Two-Shoes or a teacher's pet, but it's about making something out of my life so that I won't regret it when I sway back and forth in a rocking chair years from now. Give the best of yourself and you'll realize you've accomplished something to be strongly proud of.*

Staying Committed

The remainder of therapy focused on helping Emily to stay committed to her valued life directions. Emily loved animals, and she wanted to be a veterinarian. She began to volunteer at a local animal shelter. She walked the homeless dogs and cleaned the cat litter boxes. Emily felt good providing this service. She understood her loving touch was the only human contact some of these animals had all day. When the dogs wagged their tails and the cats purred, she knew that she was making a difference.

We often pointed out to Emily that her weight did not matter to these animals. They did not care what she looked like outside; they only appreciated the loving soul inside. To support Emily's progress, we provided her with a colorful certificate with illustrations of dogs and cats that said, "Kindness to Animals Is the Hallmark of Human Achievement." Emily's father drove her to the animal shelter, which helped Emily strengthen her relationship with her father and spend quality time with him. This example illustrates the interconnectedness of valuing. Emily was providing a service (citizenship), acting on her desire to be a veterinarian (career), and working on her relationship with her father (family), all at the same time.

As Emily continued to move in her valued directions, she ate in healthier ways. Food was the fuel that propelled her bus on the valued direction route. She now had more energy to be a better athlete. She was able to concentrate better on her schoolwork. She stopped lying to and arguing with her mother. Her health improved, and her menstrual period returned.

Treatment Results

Emily completed eating disorder questionnaires similar to the ones you have completed in this workbook. At the start of treatment, Emily's most severe problems were her intense drive to be thin, feelings of ineffectiveness, and body dissatisfaction. At the end of treatment, Emily's drive for thinness and feelings of ineffectiveness were reduced to a normal level.

Her body dissatisfaction remained high. Emily still did not like the way she looked, and she would have preferred to be thinner. This is a very important result to note, and we were not surprised by it. Remember that the goal of ACT is not to help you like your

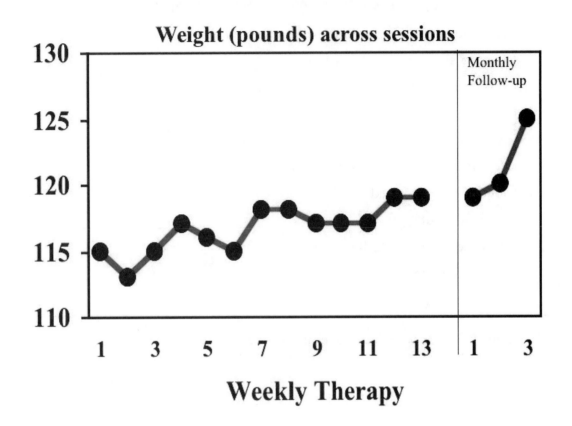

Weekly Therapy

body more. The goal is to help you live life fully and feel what there is to be felt. If those feelings include dislike of your body, then so be it. If you start to live the way you want to live and do what you really want to do, then you have succeeded, regardless of how you might feel about the shape and size of your body. This is the reason why we consider Emily's treatment to be a success: she thought she was unattractive *and* still ate in healthier ways, participated in sports, dated, and nurtured animals. Her body dissatisfaction had not changed—what had changed was her reaction to feeling unattractive.

We weighed Emily at every session. We didn't provide her with any specific weight gain goals, nor did we specifically ask her to eat more. From the graph, you can see how Emily's weight increased. Many clients with anorexia fear that they will be more miserable if they gain weight. For Emily, her life improved as she gained weight.

At our final session, we asked Emily what she thought about treatment. She said she hadn't wanted to come at first, but she was glad that she had done it. It scared her to imagine what her life would have been like if she hadn't gone through therapy.

To let us know how much she appreciated therapy, she prepared a Top 10 List, which will give you a glimpse into her writing talent and humorous personality.

Top 10 Reasons Why I See My Shrink:

10. Gives me something to do on Tuesdays at 4 P.M.

9. I love to sit on fluffy chairs forever.

8. I thrive for every session.

7. I love the opinions from my shrink.

6. Psychologist is cheaper than my phone bill.

5. Driving to the session gives my dad something to do.

4. I love getting weighed.

3. I love free stuff.

2. Saves me from calling the advice line.

1. My shrink is cool.

She signed the list with her name and a happy face.

PART III

PROFESSIONAL TREATMENT ISSUES

CHAPTER 10

Professional Treatment Options

In this chapter you will learn:

* Whether you need professional treatment

* What types of treatment options are available

* What type of treatment is best for you

Congratulations! You have completed the ACT program. Now is the time to think about where you want to go from here. To decide if you might need additional treatment, complete the self-assessment below.

Your Treatment Needs

1. What are your treatment needs?
     When you first selected this workbook, what did you hope to get out of reading it?

_____

_____

_____

_____

As you read the chapters, did you recognize any other issues, not listed above, that you need to work on?

_____

_____

_____

_____

2. Have your needs been met?
Think about what you learned from this workbook.

_____

_____

_____

_____

Which of your needs, listed above, were met for the most part or completely?

_____

_____

_____

_____

Which of your needs, listed above, were met only partially or not at all?

_____

_____

_____

_____

We also encourage you to complete the follow-up questionnaires included in chapter 14. We hope this workbook has addressed your most important treatment needs. Yet we also realize that a self-help workbook has limitations, and that you may decide you need to talk to a real, live human being about your problems. Use your answers to the questions above to decide whether there are more issues to address. If you feel that is the case, you can choose to participate in additional treatment. Congratulate yourself for making the commitment to staying healthy!

Do not avoid making a therapy appointment, especially if you think it is necessary. Some people are scared or embarrassed to be seen in a mental health setting. Others are uncomfortable discussing their personal problems and worry that they will be judged.

Here are some common reasons why clients may avoid getting the treatment they need:

- Shelby, age twenty-three: *I am desperate for help, but I never want to see a therapist. If they knew the horrible things I've done, they would think I'm so stupid. I just can't imagine being alone in a room with someone and having to reveal how sick I really am.*

- Eliza, age twenty-eight: *I looked up a phone number for an anorexia specialist in the phone book. I dialed the number, but I wimped out and hung up when the receptionist answered. Later that day, I started to call again, but I hung up before I even finished dialing. I'm just not ready for therapy right now.*

Practice what you learned in this workbook. Get off your "but"! If you think, "I want treatment, but I'm scared," say instead, " I want treatment *and* I'm scared." Take your worries, fears, and thoughts with you to the phone book, treatment center, and therapy session. Don't let those passengers in the back of your recovery bus take you off the route to a healthy life.

Who Treats Eating Disorders?

In this chapter, we describe the various treatment options available to you. We refer to professionals as "therapists." This is a general term that includes a variety of professionals, including counselors, social workers, psychologists, students-in-training, and others. Anyone can use the title "therapist," regardless of their level of training. So, you may want to check their professional title and training before you go and meet with them.

Of the many different professionals, psychologists are doctors (Ph.D.s or Psy.D.s) who receive extensive training and have been licensed by the state to treat people with behavioral problems. If at all possible, you should seek treatment from a licensed psychologist who specializes in eating disorder treatment. Be aware that not all psychologists are trained to work with eating disorder clients, so you may have to search for the right psychologist.

What Are My Treatment Options?

The first stop on your road to recovery is to decide which type of treatment you may still need. In this chapter, we'll help you to make an informed choice, and we'll prepare you to participate in treatment.

Before we tell you more about treatment options, we want to remind you that it may be necessary to contact a hospital emergency room when your life is in danger as a result of your struggle with anorexia. As we discussed in chapter 1, anorexia is the most fatal psychological condition, and you should seek help from a professional immediately if you feel your life is in danger. This is particularly true if you are extremely malnourished, or if you are thinking about committing suicide.

In-Patient Hospitalization

If anorexia threatens your survival, you may need to stay in a medical or psychiatric hospital until your condition improves. You should be hospitalized if you meet any one of the following criteria:

- Your body weight is extremely low, and you are malnourished.

- You are experiencing medical problems, such as heart problems.

- You have serious psychological problems, such as substance abuse or suicidal thoughts, in addition to anorexia.

- Less intensive treatments have not worked for you.

- You need to be in a structured, supervised environment in order to restrict excessive use of laxatives, vomiting, and/or exercise.

Typically, a doctor must initiate a hospitalization. You can't just show up at the hospital and say, "I'm here to check in." So, if you think you should be hospitalized, see your family physician or psychotherapist, or go to the emergency room.

If you are admitted to a medical hospital, the main focus of treatment will be to restore your physical health and strength. You will primarily receive medical treatment, and your psychological symptoms may not be addressed at all.

If you are admitted to a psychiatric hospital, you will have a team of professionals working to help you: medical doctors, psychologists, nutritionists, and social workers. When you are first admitted, you will participate in a physical exam and a psychological evaluation. In addition to medical evaluations and nutritional counseling, you will also participate in psychotherapy sessions, activities, group therapy, and skills training sessions (assertiveness, stress management, etc.).

Listed on the next page are several hospitals that specialize in treating people with anorexia. If you do not live near these places and you need emergency care, please contact the nearest hospital emergency room or psychotherapy clinic; they will be able to help you further.

The length of your hospital stay can vary from a few days to a few weeks. It really depends upon how much progress you make. Before you leave the hospital, a discharge planner will work with you to determine an aftercare plan. They may recommend that you participate in some of the less intensive options described below.

Day Treatment

Day treatment is less restrictive than the twenty-four-hour per day inpatient setting. Clients arrive in the morning and go home at the end of the therapeutic work day. While at the treatment center, clients participate in therapy sessions, meals, and activities, and they receive medical checkups.

You are suited for day treatment if you meet the following criteria:

- Less intensive treatments have not worked for you.

- Your medical condition is stable, meaning you do not have any severe medical complications that need to be treated in a hospital.

State	City	Hospital	Web-Site Address	Phone
Connecticut Florida Florida New Jersey New York Pennsylvania	Wilton Coconut Creek Coral Gables Ridgewood New York City Philadelphia	Renfrew Center	http://www.renfrewcenter.com/	800-REN-FREW
Arizona	Wickenberg	Remuda Ranch	http://www.christianet.com/remudaranch/	800-505-5752
California	Palo Alto	Stanford University Medical Center	http://www.lpch.org/clinicalSpecialtiesServices/COE/BrainBehavior/Psychiatry/eatingDisordersPsych.html	650-497-8000
Louisiana	New Orleans	River Oaks Hospital	http://www.riveroakshospital.com/mandj/eatingdisorders.htm	800-366-1740
Maine	Portland	Mercy Hospital	http://www.mercyhospital.com/patient/medicalcare/eatingdisorder.html	207-879-3795
Maryland	Baltimore	Johns Hopkins	http://www.hopkinsmedicine.org/jhhpsychiatry/ed1.htm	410-955-3863
Massachusetts	West Medford/Boston	Laurel Hill Inn	http://www.laurelhillinn.com/chprogram.html	781-396-1116
Oklahoma	Tulsa	Laureate Psychiatry Clinic	http://www.laureate.com/services/ed/edlaureate/default.asp	800-322-5173 ext. 5775
Wisconsin	Oconomowoc	Rogers Memorial Hospital	http://www.rogershospital.org/hospital/Eating/eating.htm	800-767-4411

- You do not have additional, severe psychological problems, such as substance abuse or thoughts about killing yourself.

Doctors Allan Kaplan and Marion Olmsted (1997) ran a day treatment program at Toronto Hospital in Canada, where they treated more than 500 eating disorder clients during a ten-year period. Most of their clients were treated for at least four weeks, and the average client participated in treatment for ten weeks. Kaplan and Olmsted report impressive treatment results. Clients with anorexia entered day treatment with an average Body Mass Index of 16 and left with a BMI of 21, which as you'll recall from chapter 1 is in the healthy range. They also found day treatment reduced vomiting from an average of seventeen times per week to once per week.

If you think you could benefit from day treatment too, contact your local community mental health clinic and ask if they offer day treatment for anorexia. Unfortunately, many hospitals and clinics that offer day treatment for general psychological problems do not specialize in eating disorders.

Intensive Outpatient (IOP) Therapy

IOP is less time-intensive than day treatment. IOP programs usually involve several hours per week of treatment. For example, clients may come twice per week for three hours at a time. The hours each week may be broken down to include family therapy, individual therapy, group therapy, educational classes, medication checks, and physical exams. Again, contact your local community mental health clinic to find out if they offer IOP programs. Try to find an IOP program that specializes in eating disorder treatment.

Family Therapy

Do you believe that family problems play a major part in your problem with anorexia? If so, it may help to include your loved ones in family therapy with you. Family therapy helps people to interact better and improve relationship problems that make anorexia worse. Family therapy will also teach family members how to best support their loved one with anorexia. Family therapy is open to anyone close to you, such as spouses, parents, siblings, and even roommates. You can participate in family therapy in addition to other types of therapy if you need to work on individual issues as well as family relationship issues.

Group Therapy

A trained therapist leads a therapy group of five to ten people who suffer from anorexia. A group typically begins by "checking in" with each participant to see how they are doing. The therapist will then lead a discussion on a topic or teach a new coping skill. Groups meet for one hour or more per week.

Some groups are "closed," which means that all members begin at the same time, and new members are not accepted until the next group forms. Other therapy groups are "open," which means a client can join at any time. An advantage of an open group is that some participants have begun to make good progress, which can be inspiring to new group members. The veterans take on a leadership role, which can be personally rewarding.

Many eating disorder groups focus on a specific topic and attempt to teach you specific skills, such as eating in more healthful ways.

Support Groups

Support groups consist of several people with eating disorders who meet on a regular basis to support and encourage each other. Probably the greatest benefits from participating in a support group come from realizing that you are not alone and from interacting with other people who are able to empathize with you.

The difference between support groups and group therapy is that support groups are usually not led by a trained professional. In fact, a support group may not have a leader at all. So, it's important to be selective about the support group you choose. Support groups are not therapeutic if the discussion spirals into a sounding board for people simply to express their problems and complain.

If you are interested in support groups, search through your community newspaper or a community calendar to see if there are eating disorder/anorexia groups in your area. Many support groups are free. If you are a college student, you can inquire if your campus offers eating disorder therapy groups or support groups through the university counseling center.

Online Support Groups

Some people prefer online support groups because this format allows anonymity and is convenient for people who are unable to locate other treatment options in their area. Some online support groups meet on a scheduled basis. All members log on at the same time and electronically interact during a set time period. Other online groups use e-mail postings and message boards that allow members to post questions and responses throughout the day.

If you are interested in participating in an online support group, you should select one that has a moderator. Although the moderator may not be a mental health professional, he or she will screen out any inappropriate posts.

Keep in mind that there are disadvantages to online support groups. Sometimes, there are people who misrepresent themselves and prey on vulnerable people. Others may post hurtful or inappropriate comments. Finally, remember that professionals may not be involved in on-line support groups, so the information quality may not be as good as what you would get from a professional.

Medication

Before we discuss medication options, we want to point out that we are psychologists, not medical doctors. We specialize in the field of psychology, which means our expertise is in the area of behavior change. We do not prescribe medications.

Only medical professionals can prescribe medication. If you have specific questions about medications, we recommend that you ask your family physician, or better yet, find a psychiatrist in your area. (Psychiatrists are medical doctors who specialize in mental health.)

We can tell you that none of the drugs that researchers have tested on people effectively treat anorexia. The general rule of thumb is that medication is not needed, and should only be used in combination with other types of therapy.

As you learned in chapter 1, occasionally people with anorexia also suffer from depression. Some people thought that antidepressant medication might treat anorexia as well. Although antidepressants may work well in the treatment of bingeing and purging for bulimia, they are only effective for anorexia after your weight has increased. The main reason is that some depression symptoms, such as irritability and concentration problems, are caused by semi-starvation, and these symptoms will persist if you are not maintaining a healthy weight. Also, some types of antidepressants are dangerous to prescribe to clients with anorexia. For instance, one type of antidepressant, called tricyclics, increases the risk of heart problems and sudden death for people with a low body weight (Zhu and Walsh 2002).

If antidepressants are not effective, what about other types of medications? Garfinkel and Walsh (1997) described how some researchers thought antipsychotic medications might work because one could argue that anorexic beliefs are at odds with reality: How can someone so thin believe they are fat? However, research has shown that antipsychotic medication does not change the beliefs of clients with anorexia, but does have the side effect of weight gain. Also, antipsychotics are powerful drugs, and in this study they led to seizures and other severe side effects in some of the people treated. Garfinkel and Walsh concluded that the risks of antipsychotic medication outweigh the treatment benefits.

What about appetite stimulants? These also are not helpful. Appetite stimulants don't work because lack of appetite is usually not a problem in anorexia. In fact, many clients with anorexia report intense hunger. Also, people with anorexia may refuse to take appetite stimulants because they fear the drug will cause them to eat or gain weight. It is just as difficult to administer an appetite stimulant as it would be to administer food. In some cases, an appetite stimulant can make the problem worse if you continue to restrict eating while taking the drug. The rewarding feeling of being in control is intensified if you "beat" the medication's attempt to stimulate eating.

What does work? Some antianxiety medications can be helpful if you have intense fears or worries. In this case, the medication is treating the anxiety, not the eating disorder. So, any benefit of antianxiety medication is indirect.

Although drugs that treat the psychological aspects of anorexia are not very effective, drugs used to alleviate some of the physical and medical problems of anorexia can be helpful. Nearly every client we treat describes how disgusting it feels to have food sitting in their stomach. Researchers have actually found that clients with anorexia have stomachs that do not empty as quickly as the stomach of the average person (McCallum et al. 1985; Domstad et al. 1987). There are some medications that can speed up gastric emptying.

In this workbook, we've described mindfulness techniques to help you learn to observe, feel, and ride the wave of your discomfort. We recommend that you complete the workbook exercises without taking medication, unless it is absolutely needed and a physician tells you to take it. We want you to practice mindfulness and be aware of even your most intense emotions. When medication dulls your emotions, mindfulness is more difficult to practice. The advantage of mindfulness over medication is that mindfulness is a skill that you can keep and take with you on your journey through life. Taking medication is not a skill. With medication, once you stop taking the pill, you are often back to where you started.

We are also concerned that you may view medication as a quick fix: If you take this pill, your problems will go away. If only life could be that simple! In a way, medication is a crutch that you could misuse to avoid dealing with your problem. The essence of the

ACT approach described in this workbook is to give up such avoidance, choose valued directions, and take action. Throughout this workbook we have therefore emphasized that you need to approach your problems and take action. A pill is not going to solve your problems for you.

Individual Therapy

In individual therapy, you meet one-on-one with a personal therapist for approximately one hour per week. For some clients, one hour per week isn't enough. If your symptoms worsen, the therapist will recommend that you participate in the more intensive treatment options described above.

Most therapists use techniques from cognitive-behavioral therapy (CBT) and interpersonal psychotherapy (IPT), the two most established types of therapy for anorexia. You can read more about CBT and IPT in chapter 11.

CHAPTER 11

Established Psychological Treatments For Anorexia

In this chapter you will learn about:

✳ Cognitive behavioral therapy (CBT) for anorexia

✳ Interpersonal psychotherapy (IPT) for anorexia

✳ How ACT compares to CBT and IPT

Unfortunately, the psychological treatment of anorexia is still in its infancy, and the progress our science has made in this area is somewhat disappointing. This limited progress was actually one of the reasons we decided to write this book. In recent years, eating disorder experts have found that cognitive behavioral therapy (CBT) and interpersonal psychotherapy (IPT) are the most effective treatments for anorexia. However, even these two treatments have been only moderately successful at best. There is simply no known "cure" or proven psychological treatment for anorexia at this point.

Right now, there has not been enough research conducted to demonstrate the value of ACT with anorexia. ACT has just made its debut as a treatment for anorexia, and we will still have to wait a few years before we have the results from bigger studies to see how well ACT works with a large number of clients. However, preliminary findings show that the ACT approach has much to offer clients with anorexia, and we hope that you too have experienced how well ACT can work.

ACT has built upon and refined CBT techniques, and it includes some elements of IPT and other treatment approaches. As you read on, see if you notice the similarities and differences between ACT and these other more established treatments. You may be interested to know that ACT evolved out of the CBT tradition, and some consider ACT to be the next wave of CBT—the new style of cognitive behavioral therapy.

In this chapter, we will detail the CBT and IPT approaches to educate you about other treatments for anorexia. If you decide to participate in treatment with a mental health professional, you will probably receive either CBT or IPT because most eating disorder therapists are not familiar with the ACT approach yet, although the popularity of ACT is growing.

Cognitive Behavioral Therapy (CBT)

CBT focuses on helping people to change their cognitions (thoughts) and behavior. CBT was originally just BT—behavior therapy. And just like its name, the focus was on changing people's behavior. Behavior Therapy was developed in the 1950s when clinical psychologists learned about experiments on animals and humans that demonstrated how behavior can be changed and controlled. The clinical psychologists decided to apply the laboratory findings to treat people with behavior problems.

The C was added to BT some years later when psychologists felt that it was time to also consider cognitions (people's thinking). We agree with this view because what people think and say to themselves does play a major role in psychological problems. For this reason, thinking needs to be addressed in therapy.

Research has shown that many people have benefited from CBT. It is the treatment of choice for many disorders, ranging from autism to anxiety. For bulimia, CBT is the best treatment available. There are a number of CBT self-help books and treatment manuals available for bulimia.

Because CBT works well for bulimia, psychologists decided to apply similar techniques to anorexia too. As you know from experience, the condition we call anorexia is really just a combination of certain behaviors and thoughts. Below are some examples.

Behaviors:

- Dieting

- Purging

- Telling lies to loved ones

- Weighing yourself frequently

Thoughts:

- When I control how much I eat, I feel that I am stronger than most people.

- No one likes fat people.

- If I gain weight, I will be a total failure.

- People like me more when I'm thin.

Eating disorder experts hoped that CBT would help people cope better with these thoughts and behaviors. Unfortunately, the results for anorexia have not been as promising as the treatment results for bulimia. Weight gain is the main goal of CBT, and many anorexic clients fear weight gain so much that they either refuse to participate in treatment or drop out before making progress. Even when clients with anorexia stick with a CBT program and do gain weight, as many as 50 percent of them relapse and go back to dieting after treatment is completed (Mizes 1995).

Despite these disappointing results, CBT remains one of the most commonly used treatments for anorexia. There are four CBT techniques that we will describe in detail:

- Food diaries

- Reward systems to increase eating

- Exposure to uncomfortable situations

- Thought changing

Food Diaries

With eating disorder clients, food diaries are often the first step to behavior change. In a food diary, a client records how much she eats, and what happened before and after eating. In CBT, this is called the A-B-C approach.

- A is for antecedents, or the events/emotions before eating

- B is for behavior, the amount of food you ate and how you ate it

- C is for consequences, or what you felt, thought, or did after eating

For example, Kylie completed the following food diary:

Date	Antecedent	Behavior	Consequence
1/16	*Went to dinner with Tim*	*Ate three bites* *Played w/my food*	1. *Felt bad b/c Tim paid* 2. *Relieved he did not comment on how little I ate*
1/17	*Home alone. Bored.*	*Ate 1 cup pretzels*	1. *Felt OK b/c they are fat-free* 2. *Fell asleep afterward*
1/18	1. *Felt Weak* 2. *Felt Conflicted*	*Ate 1 bowl cereal*	1. *Disappointed that I ate* 2. *Walked 1 mile*

The purpose of the food diary is to find out more specifically what happens before you eat and what happens afterward (the consequences). Having this information can be useful in designing programs to help you change your eating behavior. Food diaries also make you more aware of the situations and consequences that are related to eating problems. Sometimes, you can discover the solution to a problem when you know more details about the problem. The diaries can help you learn in which situations you eat and don't eat. You'll learn which situations are most and least comfortable for you, and you'll become aware of how you and other people in your life react to these situations. The diaries also provide an accurate, detailed description of how much you actually eat.

In ACT, food diaries can be useful too. When you write down your thoughts, feelings, behavior, and situation, you practice being an observer. This can be a great way to practice mindfulness. Just be sure that your intention is to observe.

Reward Systems

Reward systems provide rewards and incentives to encourage clients to eat more. The therapist helps the client prepare a list of rewards, such as money, objects, and places the clients would like to visit. Then, food goals are set. If the client fulfills the food goal, she earns the rewards. Usually, the client will earn a small daily reward and a larger weekly reward.

For example, Mary's mom agreed to pay Mary three dollars for each day that Mary drank an entire can of a nutritional shake. If Mary drank the shake each day for a week, she earned an additional five dollars. At the end of the week, Mary and her mom shopped with the money Mary earned on the reward plan. As treatment progressed, food goals were changed, and more foods were gradually added to Mary's meal plan.

The CBT reward system is a good short-term solution, but it doesn't work well in the long run. Clients sometimes revert back to old patterns once the external reward system is removed because they no longer have an incentive to eat. In ACT, we are interested in long-term progress. That is why we focus on valued living rather than short-term reward goals. The pursuit of your values is a lifelong process aimed at producing results for years and years to come.

Exposure

Exposure is a common technique used in ACT and CBT. Just as you did in chapter 6, CBT clients develop lists of uncomfortable situations. Some of these situations may be directly related to eating (such as, having dinner) and others may only be indirectly related to eating (for example, being together with a group of friends).

Just like you, if a client is dissatisfied with her body, she does mirror exposure. If she fears weight gain, she completes the scale exposure. The CBT exposure activities are very similar to the exercises you completed in chapter 6. For instance, using the same staircase approach we presented, CBT therapists also frequently ask their clients to go through and experience situations starting from the least feared to the most feared.

There are differences between ACT and CBT in terms of the manner in which exposure is conducted and the goal of exposure. Just like in ACT, a CBT therapist would ask you to approach situations you previously avoided, but at times CBT therapists will teach their clients relaxation techniques to soften the effects of exposure. In ACT, we would not make any attempt to influence or change your experience. Instead, we encourage you to approach uncomfortable situations and allow yourself to ride the wave of discomfort, fully experiencing all of your thoughts and feelings. You are not supposed to do anything except notice your natural reaction to the situation. In ACT, we emphasize acceptance of emotions. We want you to let go and give up the struggle to control your emotional state, whereas in CBT the ultimate goal of exposure is to reduce your level of discomfort.

Thought Changing

The goal of thought changing is to help you change or eliminate some of the thoughts you experience. From your own struggle with anorexia, you know that thoughts about food, body shape, and weight consume much of your mental energy.

Garner and Bemis (1982) described several different thought patterns that clients with anorexia experience: magnification, all-or-none thinking, personalization, and superstitious thinking. In the table below we provide some examples of these thought patterns as they apply to people with anorexia.

Type Thought Pattern	Definition	Examples
Magnification	Exaggerating consequences of eating, and believing that eating or weight gain will lead to catastrophic consequences.	*"If I gain five pounds, no one will ever like me."* *"When I eat, my stomach feels like it will explode."*
All-or-None Thinking	Thinking that you either have it all or you have nothing.	*"If I don't have the perfect body, I am totally gross."* *"Unless I can fit into my size-two jeans, I won't go out in public."*
Personalization	Taking things too personally, and believing that you are the focus of events that occur.	*"When I hear people laughing in a restaurant, I know they are making fun of the way I eat."*
Superstitious Thinking	Making a connection between food/weight and certain events when there really is no connection between them.	*"My mom does not love me as much as she loves my sister because I am not skinny enough."*

Which of these thought patterns do you experience? In CBT, you learn more about these and other types of thought patterns. You might also be asked to monitor your thoughts in a daily diary. Using this diary, your therapist might then teach you how to challenge your beliefs.

Here are two clinical examples of how this technique works:

- Whitney recorded a thought diary. Her record showed that "I need to weigh ninety pounds to be happy" was a common thought she experienced. The therapist asked Whitney, "Well, where's the evidence? Do other people who weigh ninety pounds feel happy? Do you have any memories of times when you weighed more than ninety pounds and still felt happy?" The point of this questioning was to examine the evidence to check the accuracy of these thoughts. The goal of this check was to help Whitney recognize the logical flaws in her thoughts and exchange the inaccurate thoughts for more accurate or appropriate ones. From that point on, when Whitney noticed anorexic thoughts, she asked herself questions to check whether there was any real evidence to confirm her thoughts. If there was no such evidence, she was encouraged to think different thoughts.

- McKenna's thought diary showed that she engaged in all-or-none thinking, "If I'm not in complete control, I feel my life is totally out of control." She learned to challenge that thought by thinking about control in terms of a continuum, in which her control over life falls somewhere between total control over life and total loss of control.

Total Loss of Control ———————————————————— Total Control
      (0 %)   (100%)

Instead of viewing control as something she either had or did not have at all, McKenna learned to think about the continuum of control. She was still in control of a certain percentage of her life, even if she was not in total control of certain aspects of life.

So, to help people get rid of certain thoughts, CBT teaches clients to deal with thoughts that disturb them by challenging the evidence for such thoughts and taking a new perspective. In CBT, the goal is to increase the "good thoughts" and decrease the "bad thoughts." ACT does not categorize thoughts into "good thoughts" versus "bad thoughts." As you recall from chapters 5 and 6, we view all thoughts simply as thoughts. They are neither good nor bad. Thoughts are just words and words are just sounds.

CBT strives to change thought patterns. You may have tried to do that yourself and perhaps find it hard to believe that these thought changing methods actually work. Yet there is some research evidence demonstrating that they can work—to a degree. Still, we share your skepticism, and we do not want you to get involved in such thought struggles. As we have said many times throughout this workbook: controlling something you essentially cannot control (such as your thoughts) only produces frustration and keeps you stuck where you are. We do understand that your thoughts need to be addressed. In ACT, we just deal with thoughts in quite a different way.

Our approach differs from the CBT approach in that we neither challenge your thoughts about your weight nor help you argue with such thoughts. Our goal is not to get rid of or change the thoughts you experience. Our goal is to help you experience these thoughts without responding to them, without agreeing to them, without arguing with them. In fact, the more you want to get rid of them, the more you have them. Instead, we encourage you to simply have them when you have them, because you have them anyway, no matter what.

ACT does not encourage thought stopping or suppressing thoughts. As you recall from chapter 4, several research studies have shown that trying to stop thoughts can backfire and cause your thoughts to increase rather than decrease. That is why in ACT, we recommend that you accept rather than suppress your thoughts.

Your thoughts are a part of you, and they come and go as they please. There's no necessity or compelling reason to fight with them. Instead, we encourage you to take your thoughts with you on your journey. If you are driving your bus, there is no point in arguing with the passengers in the back when you need to focus on driving. Likewise, you can't kick them off the bus if they don't want to leave. Besides, if you stopped the bus to carry them off, you would be wasting time that you need to reach your destination.

Interpersonal Psychotherapy (IPT)

Human beings don't just think and behave in isolation. We are very social creatures. Our interaction with other people can either brighten our day or make us feel quite miserable. In many cases, relationship problems are at the core of our psychological problems.

IPT was first developed to help people improve their relationships with other people. IPT was initially used to treat depression, by helping people to identify relationship problems and take action to improve interactions with other people. IPT for depression worked quite well and has been applied to help people with other psychological problems.

With eating disorders, researchers have found that IPT is a good treatment for bulimia. For instance, researchers Garner and Needleman (1997) have shown that clients with bulimia initially improve more quickly with CBT then with IPT, but CBT and IPT have shown equal treatment effects at long-term follow-up assessments.

There has not been as much research examining IPT with anorexia. However, quite a few therapists use IPT when treating clients with anorexia because people with anorexia frequently experience relationship problems:

- Blaire, thirty-one, election poll worker: *I wish I could have a "normal" relationship with people, but so many social activities are tied to eating. There is no way I can go out with friends and let someone watch me eat. If I go out and refuse to eat, I have to put up with my friends confronting me and asking me why I don't eat.*

- Krissy, sixteen, high school yearbook editor: *I don't date at all. No way. I'll never have an intimate relationship with a guy because I'm afraid what he'd think if he saw me naked. I can't believe there are girls in my school who are bigger than me, who sleep with guys. How can they not worry about how they look naked?!*

- Connie, thirty-five, mystery novel reader: *I am all alone, and I have no one to talk to. No family. No children. I've been divorced twice. My last husband cheated on me and made me look like a fool. That breakup was so brutal I don't even want to be involved with anyone ever again.*

IPT is all about improving your relationships, and there is no direct focus on eating. An IPT therapist is not going to set up reward systems to encourage you to eat more or plan exposure exercises to help you cope with discomfort around food. That is a difference between IPT and CBT, which is more focused on eating.

However, it is likely you will start to eat more if you participate in IPT treatment because, as your relationships improve, you'll start to feel more in control of your life. You'll want to eat to have the strength to fully participate in relationships.

In a way, IPT is very similar to relationship values in ACT. In chapter 7, you thought about the type of child, parent, spouse, friend, coworker, classmate, and sibling you want to be. You may have noticed a difference between the type of relationship you want to have versus the type of relationships you actually have. As you progressed through this workbook, we hope you have developed an action plan that can move you toward being the type of person you want to be in relationships.

CHAPTER 12

Preparing for Treatment with a Therapist

In this chapter you will learn:

✳ How confidentiality works

✳ How much treatment costs

✳ How to prepare for psychotherapy

✳ What the ACT therapeutic relationship is like

You may have selected this workbook because you wanted help, but you weren't sure if you could trust a therapist. Confidentiality is a very important part of the treatment process. Confidentiality rules establish the therapy setting as a safe place for you to talk about your personal struggles. Your privacy is also protected by a new law, the Health Insurance Portability and Accountability Act (HIPAA), which established stringent confidentiality policies that all health-care providers must follow.

Unless you sign a consent form to permit your therapist to breach confidentiality, what you say to your therapist will stay with your therapist. Your therapist cannot even acknowledge that you are being seen at the clinic. For example, suppose a mother calls our clinic to find out the name of her twenty-year-old daughter's therapist. We must tell the mother that we cannot assist her because, if her child is older than eighteen, we cannot even state that her daughter is in fact a client at the clinic.

The situation is different for clients under age eighteen because parents must consent for treatment, and they have some rights to know about their child's treatment. Sometimes, younger clients are not comfortable talking about their problem if they think mom and dad will find out about what they said. It may feel like leaving your diary out for your parents to read. If that is the case, we discuss confidentiality upfront with the client and parents at the very first session. Some parents understand that it is important for their child to talk freely during therapy sessions, and the parents promise that they only want to know about therapy discussions if their child is in danger. We work with the parents and child to define the types of "danger situations" that the parents need to know about, and we all agree that other types of topics will stay between the therapist and client.

Some clients do not want to participate in therapy groups because they are afraid other group members will talk about them outside of the group. When we conduct therapy groups, we review confidentiality with group members from the outset. First, we explain that group members are not allowed to discuss what other members say with people outside of the group.

Also, if a group member sees another member in a public setting, it is important to not acknowledge or approach that group member unless you know she is comfortable being recognized in public. It is possible that the other group member is with a friend who may wonder how you know each other or where you met. It can be an uncomfortable situation and a breach (albeit unintentional) of confidentiality.

Likewise, if you see your therapist in public, the therapist will most likely not acknowledge you for this reason. It is acceptable for you to initiate a greeting with your therapist, but you must make the first step. Be aware, of course, that if your therapist is with someone else, it puts your therapist in an awkward situation if the companion asks, "Who was the person who just greeted you?" For some clients, it hurts their feelings if the therapist ignores them in public, so it's important to recognize that your therapist values your right to privacy.

While your therapist works hard to protect your confidentiality, there are a few situations in which the law requires a therapist to breach confidentiality. Most of these situations occur rarely and involve making sure people are protected. Therapists break confidentiality in certain circumstances:

- If a child is being abused or neglected, the therapist must report this to Child Protective Services.

- If a client threatens to hurt herself or another person, the therapist may need to make referrals, warn the person who is danger, and arrange for interventions.

- A judge may issue a court order to release information.

How Much Does Treatment Cost?

Many people are concerned about how they will be able to afford treatment. Anorexia can be an expensive disorder to treat. For many people, financial problems can be a barrier in pursuit of the value of health. How can you adapt to this barrier?

Health Insurance

If you have health insurance, you should contact your insurance company to see what type of mental health benefits they provide. Find out if your insurance company requires pre-authorization of services, which means the insurance company must approve the visit *before* you attend your first appointment.

When you call the eating disorder clinic to schedule your first appointment, be prepared to provide your insurance information, and take your insurance card with you to your first appointment. If you do not have your own health insurance policy, find out if you are covered on the health insurance policy carried by your spouse or parents. If you are older than age eighteen, your parents can still list you on their health insurance policy if you are enrolled as a college student.

Confidentiality can be an issue if you are listed on someone else's insurance policy and claim mental health benefits. The policy holder will usually find out that a claim has been filed, and know that you are in treatment. If you have concerns about someone finding out that you are in treatment, please talk to the person who handles billing and insurance claims at the treatment clinic you attend.

Historically, health insurance companies have provided more coverage for medical problems than psychological problems. In the case of anorexia, that usually meant the health insurance company did not cover the cost of psychotherapy, and they only paid out if someone became so severely malnourished that they needed to be admitted to a medical hospital. Once the client was medically stable, she was discharged, often without receiving any treatment for the psychological problems that put her in the hospital to begin with. This was like putting a tiny bandage on a gaping wound.

On the brighter side, mental health coverage is improving. There is strong support for the "Senator Paul Wellstone Mental Health Equitable Treatment Act" of 2003. This law would require insurance companies to provide equal coverage for medical and psychological disorders. This means you would receive the same benefits whether your problem is medical or psychological in nature. It is interesting to note that the parity act was named after the late Senator Paul Wellstone of Minnesota, who advocated equal treatment of medical and psychological disorders and who died in a tragic plane crash. Senator Wellstone's fight to improve mental health care for all Americans is a great example of how the values he pursued in life define his legacy and memory.

How do you want to be remembered? If you value citizenship and democracy, let your voice be heard. Vote for representatives who support this act, and contact your congressional representatives to let them know you want them to pass this act.

No Insurance

You can be treated for anorexia even if you do not have health insurance. When you first call to schedule an intake appointment, the receptionist will typically ask if you have insurance or not. When you say you do not have insurance, explain your financial situation. There are several payment options you should ask about:

- *Payment plans* require that you pay the full cost of treatment, but the billing is spread out so that your payments are easier for you to make.

- *Sliding fee scales* allow you to pay a reduced cost for treatment. Your cost per session is based upon how much money you earn. The lower your income, the less you pay for treatment.

- *Charity aid* is no-cost treatment available for the disadvantaged.

If you are not satisfied with the payment options the clinic offers, ask for a referral to another clinic that provides low-cost services for people without insurance.

MediCaid

If your income is low, find out if you qualify for MediCaid, which is a government program that covers the cost of health care for the disadvantaged. You can apply for MediCaid at your state's department of health and human services, also known as the welfare office. Call first to see if you qualify for the MediCaid program, and then apply in person.

Some people are uncomfortable receiving public assistance. As we've said throughout this workbook, if this is true for you, then take your discomfort with you. You cannot die from entering a welfare office. You *can* die from anorexia. What would you rather have: Your health or avoidance of feeling uncomfortable?

Free Services

If you are a college student, find out about your university counseling center services. These services are often "free" in the sense that you have already paid for them through your student fees. Likewise, if you are employed, find out if your company has an employee assistance program that offers free mental health services.

College counseling centers and employee assistance programs specialize in treating the "worried well"—people with normal problems of living. If your symptoms are severe, these services may not be as intensive as you need. However, they can be a great resource for referrals and a comfortable, affordable way to get started with treatment.

What Is Therapy Like?

You may wonder what therapy would be like. To give you an idea, you will learn in the next section what you'd have to do to prepare for treatment and what to expect to happen during the course of therapy.

The Intake Interview

In individual therapy, you meet with a therapist for approximately one hour per week. The first session is an introductory meeting in which the therapist will gather information about you and decide if the treatment they provide can match your needs.

Although the therapist will ask most of the questions, the session is collaborative, and your therapist will welcome your input and questions. Remember, your therapist is the expert on psychological treatments, and you are the expert on you. So, you both need to work together to decide the most effective treatment for you personally.

The first time we see a client, we always give the client an opportunity to ask questions. Yet, very few clients ask anything. This is your opportunity to make an informed choice about participating in therapy. Listed below are some common issues or concerns you may want to discuss with your therapist. Be sure to address the following if they are important to you.

- Tell the therapist how often you need to attend sessions (weekly, daily, bi-weekly).

- Indicate if you have a gender preference. Many clients prefer female therapists.

- If you want to involve a loved one, tell your therapist your reason why and discuss how that person's involvement could be arranged. In some cases, we meet individually with the client for thirty minutes, and then spend thirty minutes with the client and support person together. This keeps the client and loved one aware of the treatment plan and activities. In other cases, we may spend the entire session with the client and encourage the client to discuss the session or complete their homework with the support person. Keep in mind that unless you explicitly consent to involving a support person in treatment, confidentiality rules may limit your therapist from disclosing information about you to anyone else.

- If you liked the ACT approach, find out if your therapist is familiar with ACT.

- Let your therapist know that you have completed this workbook, and share what you have learned.

- List other questions you want to ask or information you want to share:

_____

_____

_____

_____

What kind of questions do you expect the therapist to ask you at the first session? Some questions will focus specifically on anorexia. Others are general questions that we ask every new client. Listed below is a sample of questions the therapist will probably ask at your first meeting. Think about how you would respond to these questions. Write your response in the space below.

Preparing for the Intake

Anorexia-Specific Questions

What is your current height and weight?

How much do you want to weigh?

Do you do anything to get rid of the food you eat (e.g., diet pills, vomit, laxatives, etc.)?

How much do you exercise?

What is your physical health like? Missed periods? Irregular heart beats?

How long has eating/weight been a problem for you?

How old were you when your eating problems began?

General Questions

Tell me about what brought you in to see me today.

How has your mood been in the last month?

Do you have any thoughts of hurting yourself? Have you ever made a suicide attempt?

Have you been in treatment before?

What was your previous treatment experience like?

How much and how often do you use alcohol/caffeine/nicotine/illegal drugs?

Are you taking any prescription medication?

Who are important people in your life? Who is your social support?

What is your relationship with your family like?

Do any family members have a mental illness?

What are your treatment goals? What do you want to get out of treatment?

In addition to the interview, prepare to complete paperwork and questionnaires, similar to the questionnaires you completed in this workbook.

The Treatment Process

In some cases, you will return to meet with the therapist in a week or two after the interview. However, there is the possibility that your therapist will refer you to see someone else who can provide more appropriate services. If this happens, don't be discouraged. A referral is a good sign that a therapist is not trying to go in over their head and is aware of their personal limits. Not all therapists are trained to treat anorexia, and a therapist is looking out for your best interests if they refer you to someone more qualified.

After the first introductory meeting, you and your therapist work as a team. In most cases, the treatment process begins with helping you to feel comfortable with therapy. You'll spend the first few weeks building rapport with the therapist and becoming more willing to make changes and take action. You will probably be asked to complete homework assignments and work toward goals and values.

Homework is the most important part of individual therapy. You only meet for one hour per week with your therapist, and just talking about problems for fifty minutes each week will not solve much. You must take action to get results. Homework is the best way for you to create change where change is most needed: in your real-life environment.

Each time you meet, you will step on a scale for a weigh-in. Your therapist needs to know your body weight because your therapist is responsible for monitoring your health. This may be uncomfortable for you, whether you are someone who weighs yourself frequently or someone who never goes near a scale.

The weigh-in is a great opportunity for you to practice mindfulness. Observe the number as a number. Observe the thoughts and feelings that you associate with that number. Experience the experience, and ride the wave of your discomfort.

After several weeks of progress, you and your therapist will focus on maintaining the gains you have made. You will prepare to be your own therapist! Saying goodbye can be tough for both clients and therapists. You will have worked together for several months by that time, and you will have grown personally, in part as a result of the therapeutic relationship. Do not drop out prematurely and avoid addressing this ending. Your therapist will help you to have a positive ending and transition out of therapy.

Many of the clients we treat have appreciated their therapy experience and expressed their gratitude for the services they received:

- Pat, nineteen, college student: *I just wanted to take this opportunity to thank you for all of your help in the past few months. To be completely honest, I wasn't too certain how the entire counseling process would benefit me, but I am now so happy that I continued to give it a shot. The people I spend a great deal of time with have noticed the marked difference and change in my demeanor. I know they are much happier with my behavior now. I want to thank you especially for helping me hold together and improve my relationship with my mom. She is the most important person in my life.*

- Violet, twenty-four, office clerk: *I found out that treatment is about learning to live. I no longer feel like an empty shell. I strive each day to lead a life that works for me, a life based on my values, dreams, talents, and limitations.*

Working with Your Treatment Team

To recover from anorexia, you may need a team of professionals. Your therapist will help you deal with the psychological component, a medical doctor will help you with the physical component, and a nutritionist/dietician will help you with the nutritional component. This team will work together and consult with each other.

You are probably familiar with what a medical doctor does, but you most likely have never worked with a nutritionist and may wonder what that experience is like. A nutritionist educates you about healthy eating habits and prepares a meal plan to help you become healthier and stronger. At your first meeting, the nutritionist will gather a diet history and ask you about what foods you like, dislike, and how much you eat. Then, the nutritionist will develop a meal plan specifically for you.

Usually, meal plans start with a low calorie diet (1200-1500 calories) to introduce food gradually and allow your body to adjust to an increasing caloric intake. Eventually, your meal plan will include 3000 to 4000 calories per day to help you regain body weight. People who are recovering from anorexia need more calories than the average person to replenish the nutrients lost during times of starvation.

ACT Therapeutic Relationship

If you liked the ACT approach we used in this workbook, you may be interested in continuing your ACT work with a professionally trained ACT therapist. You now know how the treatment program works, but you have yet to discover how the client-therapist relationship works.

An ACT therapist will treat you as a human being, not as a diagnosis. In Chapter 1, we emphasized the difference between "the anorexic" and "a client with anorexia." An ACT therapist will help you to discover (or re-discover) the vivacious human being you desire to be. Treatment is not about anorexia. It's about you.

An ACT therapist will not judge you, lecture you, or put you to shame. We try to put ourselves in your shoes. We know that if we experienced the same situations and life events you have, we might behave like you do.

We do not take the upper hand in the relationship. We work together, as a team. Commonly, we complete activities together. Together, we observe, eat, and stick our fingers in Chinese finger traps. Obviously, ACT therapists are quite active in the session. ACT is all about taking action, and ACT therapists practice what they preach.

You'll see us put acceptance into action. We will accept you as you are. We don't impose our values on you or force you to do anything. You're the driver of your own bus, and we merely help you plan the route you want to take.

A Final Note About Treatment

You did it! You have now reached one of the last paragraphs in the main part of this workbook. It's time to give yourself a pat on the back and celebrate your achievement.

Completion of this workbook may have been a goal you set in pursuit of the value of health. We encourage you to keep moving toward your other values as well.

Although you have finished reading this workbook, your work is not done. Recovery is a life-long journey, and we hope you have learned how to ACT. Keep driving your bus in a valued direction, no matter what passengers you pick up along the way. Enjoy the new opportunities that await you in life.

"What appears to be an end may really be a new beginning."

PART IV

ADDITIONAL
RESOURCES

CHAPTER 13

A Chapter for
Loved Ones

In this chapter you will learn:

* About normal reactions to loving someone with anorexia

* How you can ACT to help your loved one

* How loved ones can be involved in therapy

Loved ones play an important role in the treatment and recovery of clients with anorexia. The family is usually the first to intervene, as they support and encourage their loved one long before a psychologist even gets involved. When clients with anorexia enter the door of the therapy clinic, it's usually because a family member set up the initial appointment, often despite the reluctance of the person with anorexia. Your role is vital.

In this chapter, we use the word "family" as a general term to describe anyone who cares about a person with anorexia: parents, grandparents, spouses, siblings, cousins, aunts, uncles, children, coworkers, friends, lovers, and anyone else that the person with anorexia deems to be an important support person.

If your loved one with anorexia has given you a copy of this chapter or book, appreciate the gift you have just received. You may have tried and tried to reach out to her, and now she is reaching back to you. This may be the day you have waited a long time for.

We hope this chapter provides you with the encouragement and advice you need to continue supporting your loved one. You also may be interested in reading chapter 1, which describes the diagnosis of anorexia, and chapters 10, 11, and 12, which describe treatment options beyond working though this workbook and also include tips on how to prepare for professional treatment. Additionally, there are several self-help books and

Internet support groups devoted exclusively to helping family members of clients with eating disorders.

Normal Reactions to Loving Someone with Anorexia

Family members work hard to help clients with anorexia. In fact, sometimes it may feel as if you are working harder than your loved one. Sadly, your concern for your loved one may be a source of suffering for you. If you've never met other families of clients with anorexia, you may feel as if no one understands the struggle you endure.

The first point we want to convey is that you are not alone. Other families share your pain. Other families have been torn apart by anorexia. We often detect this suffering when family members tell us about what it is like caring for someone with anorexia. You may recognize some of these feelings as well.

Guilt

- Bob, forty-eight, dad: *I am the father, the protector, and I feel as if I have failed my child. I wonder why I didn't see the signs of anorexia sooner. I think of all the things I did wrong as a parent that must have caused my child to do this.*

Anger

- Norma, forty-one, mom: *She has made my life a living hell. I am so mad. I love my daughter, but sometimes I hate her for what she has done to our family. It is tearing us apart emotionally, and we are going broke from all the doctor's costs.*

Frustration

- Ricky, twenty-one, boyfriend: *It is so hard to watch someone you love spiral out of control and destroy her life. I try to be supportive. I tell her repeatedly, "You are okay. You are so beautiful. You are the most wonderful person in the world to me." Nothing gets through. I want to scream because I don't know what else I can say to get her to believe me.*

Resentment

- Brent, fourteen, brother: *I missed out on a lot of stuff because my sister was so sick with anorexia. My parents ignored me because they spent all their time taking her to doctor's appointments and taking care of her. I had to quit the softball team because my parents didn't have time to drive me to practice. It's so not fair. When I need something, I can't have it because my sister gets all the attention.*

Fear

- Carolyn, twenty, roommate: *I was so scared that we would lose her. I knew she could die from anorexia. I hardly ever slept, and I got up several times each night to walk into her room and check that she was still alive.*

Your Story

Describe the thoughts and feelings that arise for you. What has it been like to care for someone with anorexia?

_____

_____

_____

_____

Guilt Keeps You Stuck

Do you wonder whether you did something wrong to cause your loved one to develop anorexia? Our minds feed us thoughts of guilt when we feel we are responsible for the suffering we experience. In your case, you may feel responsible that your loved one developed an eating disorder. You may be interested in knowing that the word responsible was originally written "response-able." The skills you learn in this chapter will equip you with the "ability to respond." Although you cannot change the past or prevent your mind from serving you thoughts of guilt, you can choose how you will act in this moment.

We encourage you to focus on the here and now. Focus on what you can do today because you can control what happens today. Unfortunately, you can't control what has happened in the past. Some family members devote a lot of energy asking, "What if I had done this or that differently?" The problem with asking "What if...?" is that you will never know the answer. That is why we focus on what *is*, not what *if*.

In Chapter 1, we discuss some possible causes of anorexia. We conclude that section by emphasizing that it ultimately doesn't matter how your loved one developed anorexia. It is like contracting the flu. It does not help you to find out how or where you contracted it. The main concern is what you need to do *now* to heal yourself, be it bed rest or taking cold medicine. You do not have to understand every aspect of the flu problem as long as you are willing to do something about it now. Likewise, you do not need to know every cause of your loved one's eating problems as long as you are willing and able to respond right now.

ACT to Help Your Loved One

In the following sections, we will provide you with some tips we have emphasized throughout this Acceptance and Commitment Therapy (ACT) workbook. These points can help you learn how to deal with your own suffering and support your loved one at the same time.

Experience Your Emotions

Throughout this book, we have described the dangers of suppressing emotions and thoughts. You may feel as if you need to be the strong one and that you can't cry or show emotions. In chapter 4, we describe several research studies showing that people who avoid experiencing emotions often feel worse, not better, in the long run.

Emotions ebb and flow, like a wave in the ocean. They slowly build up, get more and more intense, and appear bigger and bigger. Eventually, the wave will reach its peak, crash down, and drift away. Emotions come and go in a similar way. They don't last forever, even if it feels like they will. We encourage you to ride the wave of your discomfort. Allow your emotions to run their natural course. Otherwise, if you try to stop the wave, you will get caught in the undertow. So, if you feel sad, allow yourself to cry. Caring about someone with anorexia is heartbreaking, and crying is a normal reaction to your situation. Let yourself experience the wave of sadness.

Likewise, if you feel angry, notice your reactions. Notice how your body responds when you are angry. Feel your heart beating faster. Notice how your fists clench. Listen to your angry thoughts. Remember that there is a difference between feeling anger and acting on anger. Often, when you take the time to feel your anger, you will not need to act on your anger.

If you would like more information about accepting and experiencing emotions, we recommend that you read chapter 5, which includes mindful observation exercises that can help you to be an observer of your reactions and ride the wave of your emotions.

To get you started, you may wish to use the following worksheet the next time you experience an intense emotion: guilt, anger, frustration, sadness, fear, or whatever your feelings serve up. Take a time-out to complete this observation exercise. If you are a parent, you probably still remember how you used to put your child in time-out when she was young to help her cool off. Now that she is older, you need to put yourself in time-out when you experience these strong emotions. So, take a time-out and ride the wave of your discomfort.

Observing Intense Emotions

Name the Emotion(s) You Are Experiencing:

_____

_____

_____

_____

How is your body reacting? Scan yourself from head to toe.

- Notice how your forehead, neck, and shoulders feel

- Notice how you are breathing

- Feel your heart beating

- Observe your hands, fingers, legs, and toes

- Notice any sensations in your stomach

- Listen to the thoughts running through your head. Write down what your thoughts are saying to you:

_____

_____

_____

Just notice your thoughts and feelings. Don't try to stop them from occurring. Allow yourself to ride the wave of your discomfort. Allow it to build up, and get more and more intense. Then, allow it to pass.

Let Go of the Struggle

Throughout this workbook, we refer to the serenity creed: *"Accept with serenity what you cannot change, have the courage to change what you can, and develop the wisdom to know the difference between the two."*

Those inspiring words are easier said than done. Many families we work with are distressed because they have not learned to accept what they cannot change: their loved ones' behavior. These families feel trapped in a battle.

Some families devote much energy to fighting the war with anorexia. They supervise their loved one's eating at every meal. They alter what, when, and where the whole family eats. They prevent their loved one from using the bathroom after eating. They search their loved one's room for diet pills and laxatives.

Despite all this effort, the family is losing this battle. The more they try to get their loved one to eat, the more she starves herself. In some cases, the family's well-intentioned effort can backfire, and the anorexia can worsen because the person with anorexia feels a heightened sense of achievement and control if she is able to "beat" the family's intense efforts to get her to eat more.

Throughout this workbook, we discuss how futile it is to argue with anorexia. In chapter 3, we refer to it as a tug-of-war, with two teams pulling against each other. Your interaction with your loved one may feel like this tug-of-war.

Ending the Tug-of-War

How can a tug-of-war end? How can it be resolved? Most people think there are only two possible endings: either the right team wins by pulling harder than the left team *or* the left team wins by pulling harder than the team on the right side. Either way, the teams will fight until one of them has worn out the other. They will spend all their energy fighting each other. It seems they are doomed to fight until the end, right?

You may wonder, "What does all that have to do with my loved one and anorexia?" We'll give you a hint. Imagine the team on the left is your loved one's anorexia. Now imagine that the team on the right is you and your efforts to prevent her from dieting, purging, telling lies, or weighing herself. The more you pull to get your loved one to recover, the more anorexia pulls back. How is this tug-of-war battle going to end?

You can keep pulling and pulling in an endless and exhausting battle or you can do something different. You can do something that most people typically do not think of because they are busy fighting the other team. This solution may surprise you too. You could simply drop the rope!

Just imagine what would happen if you refused to fight anymore and just dropped the rope? The fight would stop in an instant. All team members would still be there and the fight would be over. You simply drop the rope . . . you just let it go . . . imagine you stop trying to pull your loved one into recovery.

We understand that you really would prefer to win. Unfortunately, you are not winning and neither is your loved one. How many months and years are you willing to drag this battle out? How much energy are you going to devote to winning this battle every day, every month, every year, again and again?

Imagine what would happen if instead of fighting you just refused to fight the battle. Imagine ending the tug-of-war. What would that be like? What would it feel like? What could you do instead with all your energy that is no longer directed at getting your loved one to eat?

When we work with families, we recommend that they drop the rope and end the struggle. It is time to let go. This means that families no longer focus on food, weight, or appearance at all. No more supervised meal times. No more reminders to eat lunch. No more third-degree questions about how much your loved one ate today. No comments about how attractive she looks (or doesn't look).

This is by far the most difficult treatment recommendation for families to understand and follow through with. Yet it is very important to change your strategy, for the reasons we describe above. We will once again stress the reasons why we recommend that you let go of the rope and end the struggle to get your loved one to eat:

- Your loved one's anorexia may worsen if she feels a sense of achievement for "beating" your best efforts to get her to eat.

- Each time you pull for eating, your loved one pulls back harder to diet.

- Your efforts are time-consuming and emotionally exhausting for you and her.

You need to turn food issues back over to your loved one or your loved one's treatment team (if she sees a professional). Let's look at both scenarios. If your loved one is not in treatment, she may have started to work through this workbook and embarked on her way to recovery. Encourage her to continue with the exercises, and avoid talking about eating or appearance. Give her some time to learn to deal with food issues herself.

If she already is in treatment, let go of the rope and let the treatment team do its job. If she is not in treatment, and you feel she should be, find an eating disorder clinic and let go of the rope. If she mentioned she would like to see a professional or if she continues to lose weight, we encourage you to read chapters 10 and 11 in this workbook to help her decide which treatment option might be best for her. Perhaps you and she can decide together which professional might be best suited for her and you can then take her to see that person.

For some families, it is both frightening and disappointing when we recommend that they stop trying to get their loved one to eat more. They are frightened and do not want the person to lose more weight. They want to help, and they initially believe that making their loved one eat more is the best way to help. It is not.

When we suggest that they turn eating issues over to their loved one or a professional, they sometimes feel that they've failed or given up. That's not true. In chapter 6, we discuss *active acceptance*. Active acceptance is the part of the serenity creed about acceptance of what you cannot change. Your loved one's behavior is one thing you cannot control or change. Understanding that and acting accordingly is very different from a passive, "I-give-up" response.

Active acceptance means you must be willing to let go and experience the fear, guilt, risk, and other emotions that come along with dropping that rope. By adopting this type of acceptance approach, you free up a lot of energy and time.

So, we have recommended what not to do. If you don't focus on eating and food, what can you do instead? We know you really want to help, so we have included some suggestions below to help you learn what you can do now that active acceptance has liberated you.

Listen and Describe

Instead of arguing, challenging, or questioning what your loved one says or does, we recommend that you describe. Let us give you an example of what we mean.

Suppose your loved one says: "I need to lose five more pounds."

An argument or challenge would be: "No you don't. You're thin enough."

A question would be: "Why do you want to do that?

A description would be: "You seem concerned about what you see on the scale."

If you question or argue, you are not listening. You are discounting what your loved one said, and you are pulling. If you say, "No, you don't. You're thin enough," we can guarantee your loved one will pull back with, "No, I'm not." Then, you throw your hands in the air in exasperation, and the communication ends. Whenever you say or imply the following words, you are arguing or questioning:

- No
- Don't
- That's not true
- Why?
- That's stupid

On the other hand, when you listen and describe, you are inviting your loved one to communicate with you. A description is an observation or a paraphrase of what your loved one said. When you describe what you hear, you show that you are really listening.

If you say, "You seem concerned about what you see on the scale," how would your loved one respond? Well, she might say, "Yes. It's hard to believe how much my life is tied to that scale." She may say, "Yes. I've had this concern for a long time." She may say any number of things, but the most important thing is that she will feel that you understand her, that you are willing to listen to her and not argue or discount her.

If you catch yourself questioning, turn it into a statement. For example, "Why would you do that?" can be turned into "I'd like to understand why you do that." You can see how the statement invites communication more than the question.

Remember that you may not agree at all with what she says or believes. However, you can understand it. You can describe it, and you can learn more about it.

When you describe, remember to give facts, not opinions. A fact can't be refuted or argued with. An opinion can. To give you an example, suppose the person says, "I need to lose five more pounds."

Fact: "You seem concerned about what you see on the scale."

Opinion: "I think five pounds is too much."

As you can see, the opinion invites argumentation and pulling, and it disrupts the communication.

We encourage you to practice descriptive communication. Use the following worksheet to create descriptive responses.

Description Worksheet

Write your factual, descriptive response to your loved one. Avoid argumentation or questioning.

Example:

Your Loved One Says: "I am so worthless."

Your Description: *People sometimes feel worthless when life is not going their way.*

Your Loved One Says: "My thighs are too big."

Your Description: _____

Your Loved One Says: "I'm not eating breakfast today."

Your Description: _____

Your Loved One Says: "I'm not very pretty."

Your Description: _____

Your Loved One Says: _____

Your Description: _____

Your Loved One Says: _____

Your Description: _____

Now practice turning questions into sentence statements.

Example:

Question: "Don't you ever hear what I say?

Statement: *I hope that we can listen to each other more often.*

Question: "Why don't you want to get better?

Statement: _____

Question: "Why are you doing this to yourself?

Statement: _____

Question: _____

Statement: _____

Support Valued Living

In chapter 9, we described the story of Emily, a young woman who recovered from anorexia. We recommend that you read that chapter and notice how Emily's family helped her. In Emily's case, her family provided support so that Emily could pursue her values.

We described valued living in chapters 7 and 8. Values are parts of life that are important to most people: relationships, career, education, leisure, health, spirituality, and citizenship. People pursue values throughout life. For instance, most people are striving to be a good friend, to learn more, etc. Unfortunately, anorexia can steer people off course and cause them to lose track of the values that are most important to them. The ACT approach helps people with anorexia reclaim their lives and values and puts them on track to start living their dreams, and their values.

We encourage family members to support valued living. For Emily, her values included a love for animals and a career desire to be a veterinarian. To move her along, her father drove her to the local animal shelter weekly so she could volunteer, and her parents were willing to tolerate the group of stray cats that Emily fed in the family yard.

You may want to ask your loved one about what she values and what you can do to support her pursuit of valued living. If you want to be one step ahead, think about a time before your loved one developed anorexia. What did your loved one enjoy doing? What was important to her before she became obsessed with food and weight?

Now, think about what you can do to encourage her to get back on track. It may mean offering to drive her to the animal shelter, as Emily's dad did. It may mean suggesting that you go shopping at the mall. It may mean that you watch a favorite movie together.

What can you do to encourage your loved one to pursue valued living? List your ideas below:

1. _____

2. _____

3. _____

Now, suggest one of your ideas to your loved one. She may say yes or she may say no. The outcome really doesn't matter. The most important point is that you do what is important to you: offering to help your loved one live a valued life. Again, you can only control your behavior, not hers. So don't try to force her into accepting your offer. If she declines, ask again at another time. If she accepts, enjoy your activity!

You can also support valued living with your language. Praise her when she moves in a valued direction. For example, if she values friendship, and she calls a friend, then tell her, "Wow! That was great that you got in touch with your friend." Be sure your praise is very specific and refers to the valued direction. Tell her exactly what you are proud of. Avoid, general praises, such as "Good job." Those will leave your loved one wondering what exactly she did well.

Be sure that you only praise value behavior. Do *not* praise weight gain, appearance, or eating behavior, as difficult as that may be for you. Remember that you have turned all anorexia issues over to her or the treatment team.

Use Person-First Language

The language you use to describe your loved one makes a difference. Many people fall into the language trap of referring to their loved one as "the anorexic." We encourage you not to label your loved one as "the anorexic" because it sends the wrong message to her and other people who know her. Instead, we encourage you to refer to her as *"a person with anorexia."*

Put the person first. Your loved one is much more than anorexia. When you refer to her as "the anorexic," it makes her and her problem one and the same, almost as if anorexia defines her. Your loved one is much more than an eating disorder. She is a vital human being filled with a lot of potential.

Case Examples

We hope you have learned some useful information in this chapter. To help you apply your knowledge, we will present two case examples. Read the examples and decide how you would handle each situation. What advice would you give to the family member?

We often give better advice to other people than we give to ourselves. This exercise is a great chance for you to practice being an observer. When you interact with your own loved one, we encourage you to take a step back and observe your interactions with her. Imagine that you are an observer or reader of your own story.

Case 1

Karla's dad was very concerned that she was not eating and was rapidly losing weight. He tried again and again to get her to eat, and he finally discovered a technique that worked. All he had to do was threaten to shoot and kill Karla's puppy. He'd never actually do it, but it seemed to work, so he continued to threaten Karla.

What is your opinion? What do you recommend?

_____

_____

_____

We recommended that Karla's dad put down the rope in the tug-of-war battle. Although he appeared to be winning now, his "victory" would eventually take a huge toll on his relationship with his daughter and her well-being.

Many clients with eating disorders feel that their life is out of control, and they use weight control as a way to feel in control again. If you threaten someone with anorexia, they will feel even more out of control and experience an even greater need to diet. Karla's dad had good intentions and wanted to help his child. He just didn't know the best way to do that. By working with us, he learned to focus less on eating and more on being a supporter of Karla's valued life journey.

Case 2

Scarlett, fifteen, high school student with anorexia: *When I am sick, everyone is by my side, and they take care of me. My mom only says, "I love you," when I am really sick. Everyone lets me get off easy. I don't have to do any chores. If I don't feel like doing something, I just cry that I am too sick. Even my teachers at school let me get away with being absent all the time.*

What advice would you give to Scarlett's family?

_____

_____

_____

Scarlett feels that her family only cares about her when she is sick. Her story is a good reminder for you to express your affection to your loved one, regardless of whether she is sick or not. Likewise, it is important that you set limits and not allow her to reap any benefits from anorexia. While we discourage you from setting limits on food or weight goals (leave that to the treatment team if your loved one needs treatment), we encourage you to be firm about your other expectations. If you are a parent, remember that you will always be the parent, and it is your job to be in charge.

It is sometimes difficult to be firm with someone who is suffering. We assume that if we just make it easier for her, then she will get better. Believe it or not, that is actually another form of pulling, and it makes your loved one feel worse. If your child was required to do chores before, expect her to do them now. If it hurts her to complete her chores because she is too weak, let that experience teach her about the disadvantages of weight loss. Of course, use good judgment, and don't expect her to complete chores, such as heavy lifting, that are dangerous for an underweight person to complete.

Our main point is that you must be firm and not allow your loved one to use anorexia as a way to reap benefits or avoid situations.

Being Involved in Treatment

In chapter 12, we offer suggestions to help your loved one prepare for her first meeting with a therapist if she decides she needs additional treatment beyond working though and acting on this workbook. We recommended that she ask the therapist how you can be included in treatment. There are several different ways you can be involved in treatment, and we suggest that you and she work with the therapist to decide which option is best for her care.

Family Therapy

Family therapy is a type of treatment in which all family members participate to improve their relationships with each other. In family therapy, family members learn to communicate better and solve family problems.

Family therapy is most useful if family problems stand in the way of your loved one's recovery from anorexia. Family therapy is especially helpful if the client is a teenager or young adult who still lives at home. In fact, some eating disorder experts believe that family involvement is necessary for treatment with younger clients to work.

If your loved one participates in family therapy, she can also participate in individual therapy sessions to work on more personal issues. She can participate in both family therapy and individual therapy at the same time.

Individual Therapy with Family Meetings

Individual therapy involves a one-hour-per-week meeting between your loved one and a therapist. This gives her a chance to have a one-on-one discussion about her personal problems. Sometimes, family members can be involved in individual therapy too.

In some cases, the therapist will meet alone with the client for thirty minutes and then spend thirty minutes with the client and family member(s) together. This keeps the client and family aware of the treatment plan and activities. The therapist may elicit the family's support to enact treatment recommendations at home.

In other cases, a therapist may spend the entire session with the client and encourage her to discuss the session or complete her homework with the support person. This approach is helpful if the family member has been too involved in the client's life. This approach will keep the family involved and also give the client some needed space and control over how much the family is involved in treatment.

Confidentiality

We discuss confidentiality in chapter 12. Keep in mind that confidentiality rules may limit how much a therapist can disclose to you. If you are the parent of a minor child with anorexia, you have the right to know what is discussed in therapy. We often discuss this upfront with the client and parents during the very first session. Sometimes, parents worry that their child may not talk about important issues if the child believes mom and dad will find out. Those parents often tell us that they only want to know about their child's sessions if we feel the child is in danger.

The situation changes drastically once your child becomes an adult. At that point, you do not even have the right to know whether your child is in treatment. You can participate in treatment only if your loved one consents.

Please note that the therapist may not be allowed to disclose anything to you, but the therapist can always receive information from you. If you feel you can provide helpful information to the therapist, send a letter or leave a message.

Now that you have learned some ways to support and help your loved one, it is time to put this new knowledge into action. Remember that you are response-able, and you are equipped to ACT to help her move in directions where she really wants to go: toward her chosen values.

CHAPTER 14

Assess Your Progress

In this chapter you will learn:

✳ To assess where you are now compared to when you started using ACT

It is useful to take a before-and-after look at yourself. As you've worked your way through this workbook, you've completed several questionnaires. You probably recall that we also recommended that you complete them again after learning and practicing the ACT techniques.

We realize that you've probably marked up the questionnaires in each chapter. That's why we have reprinted these questionnaires for you in this chapter so you can answer the questions again and see if your scores have changed. Scoring instructions are included in the chapter in which the questionnaire was first presented.

Name of Questionnaire	Chapter
MAC	2
Your Coping Style Questionnaire	4
Acceptance and Action Questionnaire	5
Values Assessment Worksheet	7

As you compare your new results to your previous results, you can see if any change has occurred. Please remember that everyone is unique, and people progress at different speeds. Some people are surprised at how much they have improved. Other people may feel discouraged if their scores have not improved as much as they would have liked. The important thing is to keep putting ACT into action for you regardless of how much improvement your results show. Remember that treatment is a lifelong journey. There is a good chance that your scores will improve over time as long as you stick with your exercises and valued journey. It may also be a good idea to go back to some of the chapters to review some of the materials—particularly if your scores have not changed at all. If you think you need professional treatment, please refer to chapters 10 and 11.

Also, keep in mind that these questionnaires only assess a snippet of your progress. You may have made impressive gains in areas that these questionnaires do not tap.

MAC Questionnaire

See chapter 2 for instructions, scoring, and interpretation.

		Strongly Disagree	Moderately Disagree	Neither Agree Nor Disagree	Moderately Agree	Strongly Agree
1.	I feel victorious over my hunger when I am able to refuse sweets.	1	2	3	4	5
2.	No matter how much I weigh, fats, sweets, breads, and cereals are bad food because they always turn into fat.	1	2	3	4	5
3.	No one likes fat people; therefore, I must remain thin to be liked by others.	1	2	3	4	5
4.	I am proud of myself when I control my urge to eat.	1	2	3	4	5
5.	When I eat desserts, I get fat. Therefore, I must never eat desserts so I won't be fat.	1	2	3	4	5
6.	How much I weigh has little to do with how popular I am.	5	4	3	2	1
7.	If I don't establish a daily routine, everything will be chaotic and I won't accomplish anything.	1	2	3	4	5
8.	My friends will like me regardless of how much I weigh.	5	4	3	2	1

9.	When I am overweight, I am not happy with my appearance. Gaining weight will take away the happiness I have with myself.	1	2	3	4	5
10.	People like you because of your personality, not whether you are overweight or not.	5	4	3	2	1
11.	When I eat something fattening, it doesn't bother me that I have temporarily let myself eat something I'm not supposed to.	5	4	3	2	1
12.	If I eat a sweet, it will be converted instantly into stomach fat.	1	2	3	4	5
13.	If my weight goes up, my self-esteem goes down.	1	2	3	4	5
14.	I can't enjoy anything because it will be taken away.	1	2	3	4	5
15.	It is more important to be a good person than it is to be thin.	5	4	3	2	1
16.	When I see someone who is overweight, I worry that I will be like him/her.	1	2	3	4	5
17.	All members of the opposite sex want a mate who has a perfect, thin body.	1	2	3	4	5
18.	Having a second serving of a high calorie food I really like doesn't make me feel guilty.	5	4	3	2	1
19.	If I can cut out all carbohydrates, I will never be fat.	1	2	3	4	5
20.	When I overeat, it has no effect on whether or not I feel like a strong person.	5	4	3	2	1

		Strongly Disagree	Moderately Disagree	Neither Agree Nor Disagree	Moderately Agree	Strongly Agree
21.	Members of the opposite sex are more interested in "who" you are rather than whether or not you are thin.	5	4	3	2	1
22.	If I gain one pound, I'll go on and gain a hundred pounds, so I must keep precise control of my weight, food, and exercise.	1	2	3	4	5
23.	I rarely criticize myself if I have let my weight go up a few pounds.	5	4	3	2	1
24.	I try to attract members of the opposite sex through my personality rather than by being thin.	5	4	3	2	1

MAC Follow-Up Results

Review the scoring directions we provide in chapter 2 and write your scores in the table below.

MAC Section	Scores Before	Scores Now
Total Score		
Weight Regulation Score		
Approval Score		
Self-Control Score		

Have your scores increased, decreased, or remained the same?

If your scores are lower now, this means you are not experiencing anorexic thoughts as often or intensely as before. If your scores are not lower now, that is fine too. Indeed, we would not be very concerned if your scores on this questionnaire have not changed much. There is no guarantee that your anorexic thoughts will ever disappear. Keep in mind that the main goal of ACT is not to change or eliminate your anorexia-related thoughts, but to help you deal with them in a different way.

Regardless of your actual score, we encourage you to continue mindful observation of your thoughts and practice the mindfulness exercises we presented in chapter 5. At the same time, we hope that you have begun to change your behavior in terms of moving in valued directions, even if your thoughts have not changed. While you're moving in that direction take whatever thoughts and feelings with you that come along and hop on your bus. Take note of them, observe them *and* do not let them steer you off course.

Your Coping Style Questionnaire

See chapter 4 for instructions, scoring, and interpretation

_____ 1a. Painful moments will hurt you if you don't do something to get rid of them.

_____ 1b. Painful moments can't hurt you, even if they feel bad.

_____ 2a. When painful moments occur, the goal is to do something to get them under control so they hurt less.

_____ 2b. It causes problems to try to control painful moments. The goal is to let them be there, and they will change as a natural part of living.

_____ 3a. The way to handle painful moments is to understand why I'm having them, and then use that knowledge to eliminate them.

_____ 3b. The way to handle painful moments is to notice they are present without necessarily analyzing or judging them.

_____ 4a. The way to be "healthy" is to learn better and better ways to control and eliminate painful moments.

_____ 4b. The way to be "healthy" is to learn to have painful moments and to live effectively with them.

_____ 5a. Being unable to control or eliminate a painful moment is a sign of weakness.

_____ 5b. Needing to control a painful moment is a problem.

_____ 6a. Painful moments are a clear sign of personal failure.

_____ 6b. Painful moments are an inevitable part of living.

_____ 7a. People who are in control of their lives can control how they react and feel.

_____ 7b. People who are in control of their lives do not need to control how they react and feel.

Your Coping Style Questionnaire Follow-Up Results

Review the scoring directions we provide in chapter 4 and write your scores in the table below.

Coping Style	Scores Before	Scores Now
Option A Total		
Option B Total		

Have your scores changed? We have found that as clients progress through the ACT program, they notice that the number of times they select Option A decreases, and the number of times they select Option B increases. This may have happened for you, too. Again, we would not be concerned if your numbers have not changed much. Change frequently occurs slowly, and any change in the right direction (no matter how small) is a positive development and a good move. Regardless of how much your actual scores have changed, please remember how important it is to stay the course and give yourself and the program time to work. Good things often do take time!

Acceptance and Action Questionnaire

See chapter 5 for instructions, scoring and interpretation.

Part I. Willingness

Statement	Never True	Very Rarely True	Seldom True	Some-times True	Fre-quently True	Almost Always True	Always True
I try to suppress thoughts and feelings that I don't like by just not thinking about them.	7	6	5	4	3	2	1
It's okay to feel depressed or anxious.	1	2	3	4	5	6	7
I try hard to avoid feeling depressed or anxious.	7	6	5	4	3	2	1
If I could magically remove all the painful experiences I've had in my life, I would do so.	7	6	5	4	3	2	1
I rarely worry about getting my anxieties, worries, and feelings under control.	1	2	3	4	5	6	7
Anxiety is bad.	7	6	5	4	3	2	1
I'm not afraid of my feelings.	1	2	3	4	5	6	7

Part II. Action

Statement	Never True	Very Rarely True	Seldom True	Some-times True	Fre-quently True	Almost Always True	Always True
I'm in control of my life.	1	2	3	4	5	6	7
In order for me to do something important, I have to have all my doubts worked out.	7	6	5	4	3	2	1
If I get bored with a task, I can still complete it.	1	2	3	4	5	6	7
Worries can get in the way of my success.	7	6	5	4	3	2	1
I should act according to my feelings at the time.	7	6	5	4	3	2	1
I am able to take action on a problem even if I am uncertain what is the right thing to do.	1	2	3	4	5	6	7
If I promised to do something, I'll do it, even if I later don't feel like it.	1	2	3	4	5	6	7
When I feel depressed or anxious, I am unable to take care of my responsibilities.	7	6	5	4	3	2	1
Despite doubts, I feel as though I can set a course in my life and then stick to it.	1	2	3	4	5	6	7

Acceptance and Action Questionnaire Follow-Up Results

Review the scoring directions we provide in chapter 5 and write your scores in the table below.

AAQ Scale	Scores Before	Scores Now
Part I. Willingness Score		
Part II. Action Score		

Have your scores increased, decreased, or remained the same? As people progress through the ACT program, their willingness and action scores often increase. That means they are more willing to experience thoughts and feelings, and take action, even if thoughts and feelings try to discourage them. The important thing is not so much the actual amount of change but that there is a change at all, no matter how small it is. Even a small step in the right direction is still a step in the right direction.

As with the other questionnaires, we would like to caution you not to expect too many changes too fast. It is okay for things to move slowly as long as you keep moving in the right directions.

Values Assessment Worksheet

See chapter 7 for instructions, scoring and interpretation.

Domain	Importance (0 to 2)	Action (0 to 2)	Match (importance x consistency)	Add to Plan?
Sample:	*2*	*1*	*2*	✓
Family				
Helping family members				
Attending family functions				
Spending quality time with family				
Strong connection with family				
Being a good/devoted daughter				
Friends				
Sharing good and bad news with friends				
Trusting other people with my secrets				
Doing fun activities with friends				
Supporting friends who need help				
Meeting someone new				
Romantic Relationships/Marriage				
Planning a date				
Expressing affection				
Having a loving relationship				
Commitment				
Companionship				

Education

Learning more about a topic I enjoy				
Achievement: Passing/Getting a good grade				
Solving problems				
Reading a book				
Doing activities that challenge me				

Career

Earning a paycheck				
Doing a good job at work				
Helping others for a living				
Doing what I enjoy for a living				
Job security				

Leisure

Having a hobby				
Participating in or watching sports				
Listening to music I like				
Doing meditation or relaxation				
Joining or participating in a club				

Spirituality

Communing with nature				
Participating in organized religion				
Having faith				
Supporting my faith (e.g., prayer, fasting, meditation)				
Feeling connected to a higher power				

Domain	Importance (0 to 2)	Action (0 to 2)	Match (importance x consistency)	Add to Plan?
Citizenship				
Volunteering				
Educating others				
Expressing my political views				
Protecting the earth				
Feeling patriotic				
Health				
Feeling rested/Getting a good night's sleep				
Wanting to live a full life				
Taking care of my body				
Willingness to seek professional help				
Being mentally healthy				

Values Assessment Worksheet Follow-Up Results

Review the scoring directions we provide in chapter 7 and write your scores in the table below:

Values Assessment	Scores Before	Scores Now
Importance		
Action		
Match		

Have your scores changed? As people progress through the ACT program, they often notice that they can identify an increased number of important values (increased importance score). They also take action more often (increased action score). Finally, there may be a better match between their values and their behavior (increased match score).

As with the other questionnaires, we would again like to caution you not to expect too many changes too fast. It is okay if your progress is slow as long as you keep moving in the right directions. This is a journey that will continue for a lifetime. Yes, it's true that you do not want to waste valuable time. At the same time, you also do not want to push too hard for change. Learn to be patient. It is fine if you feel disappointed or somewhat discouraged. Take those feelings of disappointment and discouragement with you on your bus *and* keep moving in the right directions—the directions you value. Just don't let those old all-too-familiar passengers tell you where to take your bus.

References

Albers, S. 2003. *Eating Mindfully*. Oakland, Calif.: New Harbinger.

American Psychiatric Association. 2000. *Diagnostic and Statistical Manual of Mental Disorders* (4th ed. text revision). Washington, D.C.: Author.

Barlow, D. H., and V. M. Durand. 2003. *Abnormal Psychology: An Integrative Approach (4th edition)*. New York: Wadsworth.

Bond, F. W., and D. Bunce. 2003. The role of acceptance and job control in mental health, job satisfaction, and work performance. *Journal of Applied Psychology*.

Brownell, K. D. 1991. Dieting and the search for the perfect body: Where physiology and culture collide. *Behavior Therapy* 22:1-12.

Cockell, S. J., J. Geller, and W. Linden. 2002. The development of a decisional balance scale for anorexia nervosa. *European Eating Disorders Review* 10:359-375.

Davies, M. I., and D. M. Clark. 1998. Thought suppression produces a rebound effect with analogue post-traumatic intrusions. *Behaviour Research and Therapy* 36:571-582.

Davis, M. D., E. R. Eshelmann, and M. McKay. 2000. *The Relaxation and Stress Reduction Workbook* (5th edition). Oakland, Calif.: New Harbinger.

Deep, A., L. R. Lilenfeld, K. H. Plotnicov, C. Pollice, and W. H. Kays. 1999. Sexual abuse in eating disorder subtypes and control: The role of co-morbid substance dependence in bulimia nervosa. *International Journal of Eating Disorders* 25:1-10.

Domstad, P. A., W. J. Shih, L. Humphries, F. H. DeLand, and G. A. Digenis. 1987. Radionuclide gastric emptying studies in patients with anorexia nervosa. *Journal of Nuclear Medicine* 28:816-819.

Eifert, G. H., and M. Heffner. 2004. The effects of acceptance versus control contexts on avoidance of panic-related symptoms. Working paper, Chapman University and West Virginia University.

Franklin, J. C., B. C. Schiele, J. Brozek, and A. Keys. 1948. Observations on human behavior in experimental semi-starvation and rehabilitation. *Journal of Clinical Psychology* 4:28-45.

Garfinkel, P. E., and B. T. Walsh. 1997. Drug therapies. In *Handbook of Treatment for Eating Disorders*, edited by D. M Garner and P. E. Garfinkel. New York: Guilford Press.

Garner, D. M., and K. M. Bemis. 1982. A cognitive-behavioral approach to anorexia nervosa. *Cognitive Therapy and Research* 6:123-150.

Garner, D. M., and L. D. Needleman. 1997. Sequencing and integration of treatments. In *Handbook of Treatment for Eating Disorders*, edited by D. M. Garner and P. E. Garfinkel. New York: Guilford Press.

Gleaves, D. H., K. P. Eberenz, and M. C. May. 1998. Scope and significance of posttraumatic symptomatology among women hospitalized for an eating disorder. *International Journal of Eating Disorders* 24:147-156.

Hall, R. C., L. Tice, T. P. Beresford, B. Wooley, and A. K. Hall. 1989. Sexual abuse in patients with anorexia nervosa and bulimia. *Psychosomatics: Journal of Consultation Liaison Psychiatry* 30:73-79.

Harvey, A. G., and R. A. Bryant. 1998. The effect of attempted thought suppression in acute stress disorder. *Behaviour Research and Therapy* 36:583-590.

Hayes, S. C., R. T. Bissett, Z. Korn, R. D. Zettle, I. S. Rosenfarb, L. D. Cooper, and A. M. Grundt. 1999. The impact of acceptance versus control rationales on pain tolerance. *The Psychological Record* 49:33-47.

Hayes, S. C., K. D. Strosahl, and K. G. Wilson. 1999. *Acceptance and Commitment Therapy.* New York: Guilford Press.

Hayes, S. C., A. Masuda, and H. DeMey. In press. Acceptance and commitment therapy and the third wave of behavior therapy. *Gedragstherapie (Dutch Journal of Behavior Therapy).*

Heffner, M., J. A. Sperry, G. H. Eifert, and M. Detweiler. 2002. Acceptance and Commitment Therapy in the treatment of anorexia nervosa: A case example. *Cognitive and Behavioral Practice* 9:232-236.

Herrigel, E. 1953. *Zen in the Art of Archery.* New York: Pantheon Books.

Johnston, L., C. M. Bulik, and V. Anstiss. 1999. Suppressing thoughts about chocolate. *International Journal of Eating Disorders* 26:21-27.

Kaplan, A. S., and M. P. Olmsted. 1997. Partial hospitalization. In *Handbook of Treatment for Eating Disorders*, edited by D. M. Garner and P. E. Garfinkel. New York: Guilford Press.

Kessler, R. C., A. Sonnega, E. Bromet, M. Hughes, and C. B. Nelson. 1995. Posttraumatic stress disorder in the National Comorbidity Survey. *Archives of General Psychiatry* 52:1048-1060.

Lewinsohn, P. M., R. F. Munoz, M. A. Youngren, and A. M. Zeiss. 1992. *Control Your Depression.* New York: Simon & Schuster.

Luciano-Soriano, M. C., S. G. Martin, M. H. Lopez, and F. C. Luque. 2001. Alcoholismo, evitacion experiencial y terapia de aceptacion y compromiso (ACT). *Analysis y Modificacion de Conducta* 27:333-371.

McCallum, R. W., B. B. Grill, R. Lange, M. Planky, E. E. Glass, and D. G. Greenfeld. 1985. Definition of gastric emptying abnormality in patients with anorexia nervosa. *Digestive Diseases and Science* 30:713-722.

McFarlane, A. C., C. M. McFarlane, and P. N. Gilchrist. 1988. Posttraumatic bulimia and anorexia nervosa. *International Journal of Eating Disorders* 7:705-708.

Mizes, J. S. 1995. Eating Disorders. In *Advanced Abnormal Child Psychology*. Hillsdale, N.J.: Lawrence Erlbaum Associates.

Mizes, J. S., B. Christiano, J. Madison, G. Post, R. Seime, and P. Varnado. 2000. Development of the Mizes Anorectic Cognitions Questionnaire-Revised: Psychometric properties and factor structure in a large sample of eating disorder patients. *International Journal of Eating Disorders* 28:415-421.

Mizes, J. S., and R. C. Klesges. 1989. Validity, reliability, and factor structure of the Anorectic Cognitions Questionnaire. *Addictive Behaviors* 14:589-594.

O'Connell, C. F. 2003. *The impact of caloric preloading on attempts at food- and eating-related thought suppression in restrained and unrestrained eaters.* Master's Thesis, West Virginia University, [On-line Abstract]. Available: http://etd.wvu.edu/templates/showETD.cfm?recnum=3031

Paulus, T. 1972. *Hope for the Flowers*. New York: Paulist Press.

Ryan, J. 2000. *Little Girls in Pretty Boxes*. New York: Warner Books.

Stice, E. D., D. L. Spangler, and W. S. Agras. 2001. Exposure to media-portrayed thin-ideal images adversely affects vulnerable girls: A longitudinal experiment. *Journal of Social and Clinical Psychology* 20:270-288.

Stitzel, E. W. 1948. Avoiding behavior problems: Anorexia. *Hahnemannian Monthly* 83:159-164.

Suhail, K., and Z. U. Nisa. 2002. Prevalence of eating disorders in Pakistan: Relationship with depression and body shape. *Eating and Weight Disorders* 7:131-138.

Sullivan, P. F. 1995. Mortality in anorexia nervosa. *American Journal of Psychiatry* 152:1073-1074.

Wilson, K. G. 2002. *Valued Living Questionnaire Working Manual. 11-13-02.* Available from the author at Department of Psychology, University of Mississippi, Oxford, MS.

Wilson, K. G., and A. R. Murrell. In press. Values-centered interventions: Setting a course for behavioral treatment. In *The New Behavior Therapies: Expanding the Cognitive-Behavioral Tradition*, edited by S. C. Hayes, V. M. Follette, and M. Linehan. New York: Guilford Press.

Zhu, A. J. and B. T. Walsh. 2002. Pharmacological treatment of eating disorders. *The Canadian Journal of Psychiatry* 47:227-234.

Electronic Resources

Facts of Life Interview Transcript:
http://www.geocities.com/nmmc77/transcripts08.html

ACT Web site:
http://www.acceptanceandcommitmenttherapy.com

Eating Disorder Web sites:
http://www.mirror-mirror.org/eatdis.htm
http://www.something-fishy.org

Some Other
New Harbinger Titles

Eating Mindfully, Item 3503, $13.95

Living with RSDS, Item 3554 $16.95

The Ten Hidden Barriers to Weight Loss, Item 3244 $11.95

The Sjogren's Syndrome Survival Guide, Item 3562 $15.95

Stop Feeling Tired, Item 3139 $14.95

Responsible Drinking, Item 2949 $18.95

The Mitral Valve Prolapse/Dysautonomia Survival Guide, Item 3031 $14.95

Stop Worrying Abour Your Health, Item 285X $14.95

The Vulvodynia Survival Guide, Item 2914 $15.95

The Multifidus Back Pain Solution, Item 2787 $12.95

Move Your Body, Tone Your Mood, Item 2752 $17.95

The Chronic Illness Workbook, Item 2647 $16.95

Coping with Crohn's Disease, Item 2655 $15.95

The Woman's Book of Sleep, Item 2493 $14.95

The Trigger Point Therapy Workbook, Item 2507 $19.95

Fibromyalgia and Chronic Myofascial Pain Syndrome, second edition, Item 2388 $19.95

Kill the Craving, Item 237X $18.95

Rosacea, Item 2248 $13.95

Thinking Pregnant, Item 2302 $13.95

Shy Bladder Syndrome, Item 2272 $13.95

Help for Hairpullers, Item 2329 $13.95

Coping with Chronic Fatigue Syndrome, Item 0199 $13.95

The Stop Smoking Workbook, Item 0377 $17.95

Multiple Chemical Sensitivity, Item 173X $16.95

Breaking the Bonds of Irritable Bowel Syndrome, Item 1888 $14.95

Parkinson's Disease and the Art of Moving, Item 1837 $16.95

The Addiction Workbook, Item 0431 $18.95

The Interstitial Cystitis Survival Guide, Item 2108 $15.95

Call **toll free, 1-800-748-6273,** or log on to our online bookstore at **www.newharbinger.com** to order. Have your Visa or Mastercard number ready. Or send a check for the titles you want to New Harbinger Publications, Inc., 5674 Shattuck Ave., Oakland, CA 94609. Include $4.50 for the first book and 75¢ for each additional book, to cover shipping and handling. (California residents please include appropriate sales tax.) Allow two to five weeks for delivery.

Prices subject to change without notice.